D1715862

Problems in American Civilization

NATO *and the*
POLICY of CONTAINMENT

EDITED WITH AN INTRODUCTION BY
Lawrence S. Kaplan
KENT STATE UNIVERSITY

D. C. HEATH AND COMPANY
A division of RAYTHEON EDUCATION COMPANY
LEXINGTON, MASSACHUSETTS

Library of Congress Catalog Card Number: 68-19015

PRINTED AUGUST 1968

INTRODUCTION

THE SIGNING of the North Atlantic Treaty marked the first time in one hundred and forty-nine years that the United States had committed itself to a military alliance with a European country. The Treaty defied the tradition of isolationism, the longest and most honored of all traditions in American foreign policy. What were the reasons for such a fundamental change in direction? Have the expectations of the Treaty been met in subsequent years? What is the future of the North Atlantic Treaty Organization in light of the many changes in the balance of power since 1949? These are some of the questions which arise from the position of world leadership in which the United States found itself after the end of World War II.

The origins of the alliance may be traced directly to the failure of the United Nations to operate as most Americans had hoped in 1945. Instead of a world structure of peace supported by the unity of the Great Powers in the Security Council, the United Nations was paralyzed by disagreements between the United States and its former ally, the Soviet Union. Although the Russians had quickly established political control over Eastern Europe in the wake of their advancing armies at the end of World War II, the Soviet government was not content to consolidate its power behind an iron curtain of military strength. Rather it appeared determined to exert maximum pressure on Western Europe to achieve the larger goals of communist ideology as symbolized by the creation of the Cominform in September 1947. Overwhelmed by its tremendous burdens of postwar reconstruction, Western Europe lacked the psychological, economic, and military resources to resist the pressures of Soviet imperialism.

It required at least a year and a half before the United States fully accepted the notion of an Iron Curtain and even longer before it was understood that without a full American commitment to Europe there would be no containment of Soviet expansionism. George Kennan, chairman of the Policy Planning Committee of the Department of State, was the architect of the American response to Europe's weakness and Russia's threat. Kennan's advice was to restrain Soviet power by making clear the limits to which its expansion might extend, assuming that, with a show of strength by America, internal strains and external pressures would eventually sap the dynamism of communist ideology. The first public expression of the containment policy was the Truman Doctrine of 1947, a Presidential message urging the Congress to provide emergency military aid to Greece and Turkey. The alternative to such action was the probable communist assumption of control in both countries by internal subversion, since Britain was unable to maintain its former support. Military aid to Greece and Turkey was followed quickly by an ambitious program of economic assistance, the Marshall Plan, designed to rehabilitate all of Europe on the assumption that only healthy economies could resist the intimidation and blandishments of communism.

Yet the Administration was concerned about the unilateral nature of the aid programs of 1947. They appeared to violate the spirit of the United Nations, which would be bypassed and perhaps undercut by the implementation of containment. Would not the Marshall Plan or Truman Doctrine be interpreted as a confession that the noncommunist world had failed to cope with the Soviet veto in the United Nations? Even more pressing was the possible reaction of American public opinion to a policy in which vast sums of money would be given away to indigent nations, no matter what title was given to the grants. Memories of post-World War I reactions to European war debts evoked fears of an outbreak of neo-isolationism. Hence, it was important that the containment program be placed in the context of the United Nations' Charter, justified by articles guaranteeing self defense and regional cooperation (Articles 51, 52, and 53).

As it became apparent that piecemeal economic and military help was not enough to restore the economy or the security of Europe, Europeans themselves banded together in a political organization which incorporated the principles of self-help that had identified the Marshall Plan. The Brussels Pact of 1948, whereby five European nations pledged their resources to the collective defense of their territories, testified to Europe's willingness to subsume old nationalisms under a new system of international cooperation which would defend Europe and convince the United States of the wisdom of its help. In the Vandenberg Resolution of June 1948, the U. S. Senate and country proclaimed its willingness to identify America with the new Europe.

But neither American aid nor European cooperation was considered sufficient to deter the expansionist energies of the communist world. The Soviet Union had never looked more menacing than in the summer of 1948. Czechoslovakia had fallen to a communist regime earlier in the year, Berlin was under blockade,

strong communist minorities in France and Italy were posed to assume power either by ballots or by coups. Yet in this election year the Administration and its Congressional supporters from both parties hesitated to take a step that would allay Europe's insecurity: namely, a formal alliance with the Brussels Pact nations. Only after the elections were over and after the Brussels Pact had been converted into a North Atlantic alliance of twelve countries was the United States ready to sign the Treaty. To Americans the Treaty was presented less as an alliance than as a cultural and economic association, fulfilling all requirements of the United Nations. To the European and American architects of the alliance, NATO was the last, best hope of containing communism in Europe.

For two months after the signing of the Treaty on April 4, the Senate considered its merits, first through testimony heard by the Senate Foreign Relations Committee and then on the floor of the Senate itself. The official Department of State press release made the Treaty's purposes clear and simple. They were to deter aggression by facing a potential aggressor with a firm U. S. commitment to Western Europe, which — had it existed in 1917 or in 1939 — might have prevented two world wars.

The opponents of the Treaty were articulate and resourceful in their arguments. Senator Robert A. Taft, the leading Republican in the Congress, solemnly warned that the United States would be snared in the European balance of power if it should join the alliance. Another distinguished American, Henry A. Wallace, Presidential candidate of the Progressive Party in 1948, was equally vehement in his objections to the Treaty, although for different reasons. He denounced the Pact as an act of aggression, an affront to the Soviet Union which would lead to reprisals and possibly war.

Although the Senate approved the Treaty on July 21, 1949, with a decisive vote of 82 to 13, many of the questions raised during the debate over ratification continue to influence historians who try to explain the origins of NATO from the perspective of our own time. Lawrence Kaplan notes the peculiar circumstances of America's entrance into NATO by showing how the language of isolationism was invoked by administration supporters in the Senate. Armin Rappaport, on the other hand, maintains that the American action in joining NATO was truly revolutionary, a decisive turning point in the history of American foreign policy.

David Horowitz offers an entirely different view in his pungent critique of American foreign policy since World War II. He asserts that NATO was not defensive in design, but an instrument of a policy directed toward the establishment of an American hegemony over the existing international power structure. In essence, therefore, containment was a euphemism for a policy of dictating the terms of world order "from an absolute supremacy of power."

The Korean War, even more than the Soviet acquisition of nuclear weapons, forced unexpected changes upon NATO. In the first year of the Treaty, all members assumed that the strength of the alliance lay in America's promise to identify its own defense with Europe's. The many committees and boards established under the North Atlantic Council in 1949 were useful in giving each member a sense of participation in the organization. They were useful for little else — certainly not for deterring an attack upon Europe. The major deterrent was America's possession of a nuclear weapon and the enemy's recognition that the Strategic Air Command served all twelve allies.

But with the Korean conflict, the credibility of the original deterrent came into question. To ensure Europeans of meaningful American support the United States sponsored radical changes. The major change was the establishment of a NATO defense force, including an American contingent under a Supreme Commander, who would be an American general. Secretary of Defense Marshall argued persuasively before a joint meeting of the Senate Foreign Relations Committee and the Senate Armed Services Committee on the importance of an American military contribution to Europe's sense of security. Nothing less could make the containment policy believable. The year was 1951, and the lesson of Korean unpreparedness was still very much on the minds of Americans.

Robert E. Osgood notes the extent to which the fear of Soviet action, similar to the communist move in the Far East, transformed a vague treaty into a military instrument. On paper at least, NATO in the early 1950's promised to be an integrated military organization, prepared to contain communist power from Norway to Turkey with fifty divisions agreed upon at the Lisbon meeting of the NATO Council in 1952. Additionally, German military power, suitably contained in a NATO-controlled European army, or European Defense Community, would help redress the numerical imbalance between the forces of NATO and those of the Soviet Union and its allies. Much of this expected strength was never realized; suspicion of Germany doomed the European Defense Community, and

Europe continued to depend on the reality of America's physical presence in Europe rather than on the number of American troops or European troops.

Theodore H. White takes a different view of the circumstances described by Osgood. In them he sees the reasons for Europe's recovery of self-confidence and prosperity. With the help of American military support, he asserts, Europe could rest secure from communist attack.

By the middle of the 1950's the utility of NATO's military emphasis came increasingly under scrutiny. On the one hand, the apparent taming of Soviet expansionism with the death of Stalin and the rise of Europe's ability to defend itself made the military arm less necessary; on the other, the enormous power and dangers of atomic weaponry inspired both American and European critics of NATO to urge a détente with the Soviet Union. The major spokesman at the end of the decade was the same man in whose name containment had been frequently invoked: George Kennan. His Reith radio talks in 1957 became the keynote for a new term, "disengagement." In his book, *Russia, the Atom and the West,* Kennan suggested that NATO had lost sight of its mission in its preoccupation with military defense. In his view, while the incorporation of Germany into the alliance had strengthened the NATO arm, it also guaranteed the continuation of the Cold War longer than otherwise necessary. The threat from the Soviet Union, still a reality, had changed its form, but NATO had not responded to the change. German rearmament in particular was a sore point among the Soviet bloc, former victims of Nazism, and hence might be an issue on which to attempt a thawing of the Cold War, at least to the point of withdrawing troops from a direct confrontation with the Soviets.

Not all of Kennan's friends and former associates, however, were ready to follow his suggestions. Dean Acheson, a Democratic architect of NATO, spoke for the Republican administration, berating Kennan for his naïveté on the Soviet menace.

Others agreed that disengagement in Germany would be an invitation to Soviet penetration. Henry A. Kissinger, a Harvard political scientist and one of the principal academic contributors to American thinking on NATO, shared Acheson's concerns but suggested that the United States under Dulles and Eisenhower had placed too much reliance on the specific kind of military power. "Massive retaliation," in the form of the ultimate weapon was unrealistic in an age when the Soviet Union had a counterforce, when Europeans feared the use of nuclear weapons as much as they did a Soviet onslaught. To meet the Soviet power, and to match Russian manpower required the development of a sophisticated tactical nuclear weapon. Thus the attractive idea of softening of the Cold War by disengagement was met with a more sophisticated conception of atomic power and ultimately, in President Kennedy's time, a recognition that conventional forces also played a role in maintaining the balance of power in Europe.

It was also under Kennedy's administration that the President himself became the spokesman for a somewhat vague but meaningful "Grand Design," which looked beyond the military utility of NATO to its potential as an instrument of world peace and betterment through technology. Such a new concept, expressed in a number of Kennedy's speeches, most notably at Paulskirche in Frankfurt in 1963, was dismissed as mere verbiage by Ronald Steel. Spokesman for many of the younger critics of NATO, untouched by the sentiment of the Marshall Plan of the 1940's, he called on Americans to accept the end of NATO. The arguments with DeGaulle which dominated the councils of the alliance through the 1960's or the anxieties over nuclear sharing with the allies were irrelevant. Discontent with American leadership simply indicated that in Europe's eyes the Soviet threat was gone, that America had overstayed its welcome. The Europe of the mid-sixties was as strong as America or the Soviet Union and looked at both from a different angle of vision than it had ten years or fifteen years earlier.

Perhaps the most articulate voice in Washington on the state of foreign policy in general, and on NATO in particular, was that of Senator J. William Fulbright. In a speech on March 25, 1964, later published as *Old Myths and New Realities*, Fulbright attacked America's persistence in being victimized by myths, especially the myth of communism's total depravity and total power. To Fulbright, the Soviet danger was not stilled but was merely one of many problems facing any power responsible for keeping world peace. In his peroration the future of NATO seemed closer to the expectations, or at least to the rhetoric, of 1949, in which the specific means of containing communism was subordinated to the mutual benefits of a long-term identification between the United States and Europe.

CONTENTS

CHRONOLOGY

1945   JUNE 26 — The United Nations Charter signed at San Francisco.

1947   MARCH 12 — Truman Doctrine. JUNE 5 — Marshall Plan (proposed at Harvard University).

1948   FEBRUARY 25 — Communist coup in Prague. MARCH 17 — Brussels Treaty. APRIL 1 — Berlin Blockade. JUNE 11 — Vandenberg Resolution.

1949   APRIL 4 — North Atlantic Treaty. MAY 9 — Berlin Blockade lifted.

1950   JUNE 25 — Invasion of South Korea. SEPTEMBER 15 — NATO Council meeting in New York; decision for a German contribution.

1951   AUGUST 2 — SHAPE established in Paris.

1952   FEBRUARY 18 — Greece and Turkey join NATO. FEBRUARY 20–25 — EDC accepted by Lisbon Conference of NATO Council. MAY 12 — Lord Ismay appointed first Secretary-General of NATO.

1954   AUGUST 30 — French National Assembly rejects the EDC. OCTOBER 3 — London Conference: Germany joins Western European Union (Brussels Pact).

1955   MAY 6 — West Germany joins NATO. MAY 14 — Warsaw Treaty. JULY 18–21 — Summit Conference at Geneva.

1956   OCTOBER 29–31 — Suez crisis.

1957   MARCH 24 — European Economic Community formed. DECEMBER 16–19 — NATO Council in Paris: decision in favor of nuclear weapons for NATO.

1958   NOVEMBER 10 — Khrushchev announces USSR wish to terminate Four-Power agreement on status of Berlin. NOVEMBER 16–19 — NATO Council reaffirms right of Western powers to remain in Berlin.

1959   SEPTEMBER 15–23 — Khrushchev visits President at Camp David.

1960   MAY 1 — American U-2 shot down over Soviet territory. MAY 16 — Summit meeting in Paris aborted by Soviet Union. DECEMBER 16–18 — Beginnings of MLF approved at Council meetings.

1961   JUNE 2–3 — Kennedy and Khrushchev meet in Vienna. AUGUST 13 — Berlin Wall built. OCTOBER 17 — Soviet Union waives time limit for settlement of Berlin question.

1962   JANUARY 19 — "Atlantic Convention" of NATO countries endorses a Declaration of Paris in favor of strengthening the Alliance and

Atlantic Community. OCTOBER 22–28 — Missile base crisis in Cuba. DECEMBER 21 — Bahamas meeting of Kennedy and Macmillan agreeing to contribute part of strategic nuclear forces to NATO.

1963   JANUARY 21–22 — Franco-German Treaty of Cooperation signed. JULY 15–25 — Nuclear tests ban initialed by United States, United Kingdom, and Soviet Union in Moscow. NOVEMBER 22 — Kennedy assassinated in Dallas.

1964   JANUARY 27 — France recognizes Communist China. DECEMBER 15–17 — MLF deferred at Council meetings.

1965   MAY 20 — France's Foreign Minister Couve de Murville calls for reformation of NATO in 1969. JULY 21 — France withdraws troops from NATO military exercises.

1966   FEBRUARY 21 — France to assume control over all NATO bases by April 4, 1969. MARCH 9 — France to withdraw armed forces from NATO, compelling removal of NATO installations from France. MARCH 18 — Fourteen NATO partners reiterate support of military integration of forces, rejecting France's views. SEPTEMBER 14 — NATO Council selects Casteau in Belgium as new site of SHAPE. DECEMBER 13–16 — Council meetings produce new emphasis on political and economic cooperation with lessened emphasis on military aspects.

THE CLASH OF ISSUES

World Wars I and II demonstrate that the security of the United States is directly related to the security of Western Europe and that the nations on both sides of the Atlantic are bound together by a natural community of interests. The Atlantic Pact is a formal acknowledgement of this relationship and reflects their conviction that an armed attack can be prevented only by making clear in advance their determination collectively to resist such an attack if it should occur.

DEPARTMENT OF STATE PUBLICATION No. 3462

It is said that the Atlantic Treaty is simply another Monroe Doctrine. I wish it were. That would be much more acceptable to me than the Atlantic Pact, arms or no arms. Let me point out the vital differences. The Monroe Doctrine was a unilateral declaration. We were free to modify it or withdraw from it at any moment. This treaty, adopted to deal with a particular emergency today, is binding upon us for 20 years to cover all kinds of circumstances which cannot possibly be foreseen.

SENATOR ROBERT A. TAFT

The past destroys the chances of European recovery. A permanently militarized Europe is doomed to living on an American dole. The pact is not an instrument of defense but a military alliance designed for aggression. It bypasses the United Nations and violates its Charter in a most flagrant manner. It divides the world permanently into two armed camps. And it provocatively establishes military bases on the borders of the Soviet Union.

HENRY A. WALLACE

... NATO had, as a military alliance, its part to play, but I think every one of us hoped that its purely military role would decline in importance as the curse of bipolarity fell from the Continent, as negotiations took place, as armies were withdrawn, as the contest of ideologies took other forms. The central agency in this concept was not NATO but the European Recovery Program; and none of us dreamed at that time that the constructive impulses of this enterprise, which looked to everyone so hopeful in those days, would be overtaken and swallowed up in the space of a mere two or three years by programs of military assistance based on a wholly different concept of the Soviet threat and Europe's needs.

GEORGE KENNAN

We should not deceive ourselves. After disengagement, we would soon find ourselves discussing complete withdrawal from all European areas and, very possibly, from bases in the Far East and Near East as well. Indeed, Mr. Khrushchev has twice served warning, once in Berlin in 1957 and again in January of 1958, that this sort of withdrawal which he is talking about is withdrawal from all overseas bases. This would cut the striking power of the free world by at least a half, and, perhaps, until our missile program accelerates, by much more.

DEAN ACHESON

It seems reasonable, therefore, to suggest that the character of the cold war has, for the present at least, been profoundly altered: by the drawing back of the Soviet Union from extremely aggressive policies; by the implicit repudiation, by both sides, of a policy of "total victory"; and by the establishment of an American strategic superiority which the Soviet Union appears to have tacitly accepted because it has been accompanied by assurance that it will be exercised by the United States with responsibility and restraint.

J. WILLIAM FULBRIGHT

I. PRELUDE TO THE TREATY

George F. Kennan: THE SOURCES OF SOVIET CONDUCT

In a seminal article in Foreign Affairs *in 1947, George F. Kennan ("X"), Director of the Policy Planning Staff of the Department of State, outlined the doctrine of containment that was to dominate American foreign policy for the next twenty years. According to Kennan, the basic assumption of Communist foreign policy was the existence of a hostile outside world whose menace justified the continuing dictatorship of party leaders. Not until the world accepted Communism would the Soviet Union relax its militant posture toward the West. In light of this diagnosis, Kennan was convinced that the only course open to America was to dam the expansion of the Soviet Union by military and other means until internal stresses within Communism and external failures of an aggressive foreign policy should undermine Soviet confidence in its thesis.*

THE circumstances of the immediate post-revolution period — the existence in Russia of civil war and foreign intervention, together with the obvious fact that the Communists represented only a tiny minority of the Russian people — made the establishment of dictatorial power a necessity. The experiment with "war Communism" and the abrupt attempt to eliminate private production and trade had unfortunate economic consequences and caused further bitterness against the new revolutionary régime. While the temporary relaxation of the effort to communize Russia, represented by the New Economic Policy, alleviated some of this economic distress and thereby served its purpose, it also made it evident that the "capitalistic sector of society" was still prepared to profit at once from any relaxation of governmental pressure, and would, if permitted to continue to exist, always constitute a powerful opposing element to the Soviet régime and a serious rival for influence in the country. Somewhat the same situation prevailed with respect to the individual peasant who, in his own small way, was also a private producer.

Lenin, had he lived, might have proved a great enough man to reconcile these conflicting forces to the ultimate benefit of Russian society, though this is questionable. But be that as it may, Stalin, and those whom he led in the struggle for succession to Lenin's position of leadership, were not the men to tolerate rival political forces in the sphere of power which they coveted. Their sense of insecurity was too great. Their particular brand of fanaticism, unmodified by any of the Anglo-Saxon traditions of compromise, was too fierce and too jealous to envisage any permanent sharing of power. From the Russian-Asiatic world out of which they had emerged they carried with them a skepticism as to the possibilities of permanent and peaceful coexistence of rival forces. Easily persuaded of their own doctrinaire "right-

Excerpted by special permission from *Foreign Affairs*, XXV (July, 1947), pp. 568–570; 580–583. Copyright by the Council on Foreign Relations, Inc., New York.

ness," they insisted on the submission or destruction of all competing power. Outside of the Communist Party, Russian society was to have no rigidity. There were to be no forms of collective human activity or association which would not be dominated by the Party. No other force in Russian society was to be permitted to achieve vitality or integrity. Only the Party was to have structure. All else was to be an amorphous mass.

And within the Party the same principle was to apply. The mass of Party members might go through the motions of election, deliberation, decision and action; but in these motions they were to be animated not by their own individual wills but by the awesome breath of the Party leadership and the overbrooding presence of "the word."

Let it be stressed again that subjectively these men probably did not seek absolutism for its own sake. They doubtless believed — and found it easy to believe — that they alone knew what was good for society and that they would accomplish that good once their power was secure and unchallengeable. But in seeking that security of their own rule they were prepared to recognize no restrictions, either of God or man, on the character of their methods. And until such time as that security might be achieved, they placed far down on their scale of operational priorities the comforts and happiness of the peoples entrusted to their care.

Now the outstanding circumstance concerning the Soviet régime is that down to the present day this process of political consolidation has never been completed and the men in the Kremlin have continued to be predominantly absorbed with the struggle to secure and make absolute the power which they seized in November 1917. They have endeavored to secure it primarily against forces at home, within Soviet society itself. But they have also endeavored to secure it against the outside world. For ideology, as we have seen, taught them that the outside world was hostile and that it was their duty eventually to overthrow the political forces beyond their borders. The powerful hands of Russian history and tradition reached up to sustain them in this feeling. Finally, their own aggressive intransigence with respect to the outside world began to find its own reaction; and they were soon forced, to use another Gibbonesque phrase, "to chastise the contumacy" which they themselves had provoked. It is an undeniable privilege of every man to prove himself right in the thesis that the world is his enemy; for if he reiterates it frequently enough and makes it the background of his conduct he is bound eventually to be right.

Now it lies in the nature of the mental world of the Soviet leaders, as well as in the character of their ideology, that no opposition to them can be officially recognized as having any merit or justification whatsoever. Such opposition can flow, in theory, only from the hostile and incorrigible forces of dying capitalism. As long as remnants of capitalism were officially recognized as existing in Russia, it was possible to place on them, as an internal element, part of the blame for the maintenance of a dictatorial form of society. But as these remnants were liquidated, little by little, this justification fell away; and when it was indicated officially that they had been finally destroyed, it disappeared altogether. And this fact created one of the most basic of the compulsions which came to act upon the Soviet régime: since capitalism no longer existed in Russia and since it could not be admitted that there could be serious or widespread opposition to the Kremlin springing spontaneously from the liberated masses under its authority, it became necessary to justify the retention of the dictatorship by stressing the menace of capitalism abroad. . . .

Now the maintenance of this pattern of Soviet power, namely, the pursuit of unlimited authority domestically, accompanied by the cultivation of the semi-myth of implacable foreign hostility, has gone far to shape the actual machinery of Soviet power as we know it today. Internal organs of administration which did not serve this purpose withered on the vine. Organs which did serve this purpose became vastly swollen. The security of Soviet power came to rest on the iron discipline of the Party, on the severity and ubiquity of the secret police, and on the uncompromising economic monopolism of the state. The "organs of suppression," in which the Soviet leaders had sought security from rival forces, became in large measure the masters of those whom they were designed to serve. Today the major part of the structure of Soviet power is committed to the perfection of the dictatorship and to the maintenance of the concept of Russia as in a state of siege, with the enemy lowering beyond the walls. And the millions of human beings who form that part of the structure of power must defend at all costs this concept of Russia's position, for without it they are themselves superfluous.

As things stand today, the rulers can no longer dream of parting with these organs of suppression. The quest for absolute power, pursued now for nearly three decades with a ruthlessness unparalleled (in scope at least) in modern times, has again produced internally, as it did externally, its own reaction. The excesses of the police apparatus have fanned the potential opposition to the régime into something far greater and

more dangerous than it could have been before those excesses began.

But least of all can the rulers dispense with the fiction by which the maintenance of dictatorial power has been defended. For this fiction has been canonized in Soviet philosophy by the excesses already committed in its name; and it is now anchored in the Soviet structure of thought by bonds far greater than those of mere ideology.

* * *

It is clear that the United States cannot expect in the foreseeable future to enjoy political intimacy with the Soviet régime. It must continue to regard the Soviet Union as a rival, not a partner, in the political arena. It must continue to expect that Soviet policies will reflect no abstract love of peace and stability, no real faith in the possibility of a permanent happy coexistence of the Socialist and capitalist worlds, but rather a cautious, persistent pressure toward the disruption and weakening of all rival influence and rival power.

Balanced against this are the facts that Russia, as opposed to the western world in general, is still by far the weaker party, that Soviet policy is highly flexible, and that Soviet society may well contain deficiencies which will eventually weaken its own total potential. This would of itself warrant the United States entering with reasonable confidence upon a policy of firm containment, designed to confront the Russians with unalterable counter-force at every point where they show signs of encroaching upon the interests of a peaceful and stable world.

But in actuality the possibilities for American policy are by no means limited to holding the line and hoping for the best. It is entirely possible for the United States to influence by its actions the internal development, both within Russia and throughout the international Communist movement, by which Russian policy is largely determined. This is not only a question of the modest measure of informational activity which this government can conduct in the Soviet Union and elsewhere, although that, too, is important. It is rather a question of the degree to which the United States can create among the peoples of the world generally the impression of a country which knows what it wants, which is coping successfully with the problems of its internal life and with the responsibilities of a World Power, and which has a spiritual vitality capable of holding its own among the major ideological currents of the time. To the extent that such an impression can be created and maintained, the aims of Russian Communism must appear sterile and quixotic, the hopes and enthusiasm of Moscow's supporters must wane, and added strain must be imposed on the Kremlin's foreign policies. For the palsied decrepitude of the capitalist world is the keystone of Communist philosophy. Even the failure of the United States to experience the early economic depression which the ravens of the Red Square have been predicting with such complacent confidence since hostilities ceased would have deep and important repercussions throughout the Communist world.

By the same token, exhibitions of indecision, disunity and internal disintegration within this country have an exhilarating effect on the whole Communist movement. At each evidence of these tendencies, a thrill of hope and excitement goes through the Communist world; a new jauntiness can be noted in the Moscow tread; new groups of foreign supporters climb on to what they can only view as the band wagon of international politics; and Russian pressure increases all along the line in international affairs.

It would be an exaggeration to say that American behavior unassisted and alone could exercise a power of life and death over the Communist movement and bring about the early fall of Soviet power in Russia. But the United States has it in its power to increase enormously the strains under which Soviet policy must operate, to force upon the Kremlin a far greater degree of moderation and circumspection than it has had to observe in recent years, and in this way to promote tendencies which must eventually find their outlet in either the breakup or the gradual mellowing of Soviet power. For no mystical, Messianic movement — and particularly not that of the Kremlin — can face frustration indefinitely without eventually adjusting itself in one way or another to the logic of that state of affairs.

Thus the decision will really fall in large measure in this country itself. The issue of Soviet-American relations is in essence a test of the over-all worth of the United States as a nation among nations. To avoid destruction the United States need only measure up to its own best traditions and prove itself worthy of preservation as a great nation.

Surely, there was never a fairer test of national quality than this. In the light of these circumstances, the thoughtful observer of Russian-American relations will find no cause for complaint in the Kremlin's challenge to American society. He will rather experience a certain gratitude to a Providence which, by providing the American people with this implacable challenge, has made their entire security as a nation dependent on their pulling themselves together and accepting the responsibilities of moral and political leadership that history plainly intended them to bear.

Harry Truman: THE TRUMAN DOCTRINE

President Truman before a joint session of the Congress identified a new role for the United States in world affairs when he asked for emergency military and economic assistance to Greece and Turkey in their battle against Communist subversion. Communist-led terrorists were threatening "the very existence of the Greek state." If the United State should fail in its support, the entire western world would be endangered. So spoke the President at a moment when England was unable to maintain its presence in Greece and Turkey, and when it appeared that the alternative to American action was the arrival of the Soviet Union to a position of power in the Eastern Mediterranean.

TO insure the peaceful development of nations, free from coercion, the United States has taken a leading part in establishing the United Nations. The United Nations is designed to make possible lasting freedom and independence for all its members. We shall not realize our objectives, however, unless we are willing to help free peoples to maintain their free institutions and their national integrity against aggressive movements that seek to impose upon them totalitarian regimes. This is no more than a frank recognition that totalitarian regimes imposed upon free peoples, by direct or indirect aggression, undermine the foundations of international peace and hence the security of the United States.

The peoples of a number of countries of the world have recently had totalitarian regimes forced upon them against their will. The Government of the United States has made frequent protests against coercion and intimidation, in violation of the Yalta agreement, in Poland, Rumania, and Bulgaria. I must also state that in a number of other countries there have been similar developments.

At the present moment in world history nearly every nation must choose between alternative ways of life. The choice is too often not a free one.

One way of life is based upon the will of the majority, and is distinguished by free institutions, representative government, free elections, guaranties of individual liberty, freedom of speech and religion, and freedom from political oppression.

The second way of life is based upon the will of a minority forcibly imposed upon the majority. It relies upon terror and oppression, a controlled press and radio, fixed elections, and the suppression of personal freedoms.

I believe that it must be the policy of the United States to support free peoples who are resisting attempted subjugation by armed minorities or by outside pressures.

I believe that we must assist free peoples to work out their own destinies in their own way.

I believe that our help should be primarily through economic and financial aid which is essential to economic stability and orderly political processes.

The world is not static, and the *status quo* is not sacred. But we cannot allow changes in the *status quo* in violation of the Charter of the United Nations by

From a message of the President to a joint session of Congress, March 12, 1947. Department of State *Bulletin*, XVI (March 23, 1947), pp. 536–537.

such methods as coercion, or by such subterfuges as political infiltration. In helping free and independent nations to maintain their freedom, the United States will be giving effect to the principles of the Charter of the United Nations.

It is necessary only to glance at a map to realize that the survival and integrity of the Greek nation are of grave importance in a much wider situation. If Greece should fall under the control of an armed minority, the effect upon its neighbor, Turkey, would be immediate and serious. Confusion and disorder might well spread throughout the entire Middle East.

Moreover, the disappearance of Greece as an independent state would have a profound effect upon those countries in Europe whose peoples are struggling against great difficulties to maintain their freedoms and their independence while they repair the damages of war.

It would be an unspeakable tragedy if these countries, which have struggled so long against overwhelming odds, should lose that victory for which they sacrificed so much. Collapse of free institutions and loss of independence would be disastrous not only for them but for the world. Discouragement and possibly failure would quickly be the lot of neighboring peoples striving to maintain their freedom and independence.

Should we fail to aid Greece and Turkey in this fateful hour, the effect will be far-reaching to the West as well as to the East.

We must take immediate and resolute action.

I therefore ask the Congress to provide authority for assistance to Greece and Turkey in the amount of $400,000,000 for the period ending June 30, 1948. In requesting these funds, I have taken into consideration the maximum amount of relief assistance which would be furnished to Greece out of the $350,000,000 which I recently requested that the Congress authorize for the prevention of starvation and suffering in countries devastated by the war.

In addition to funds, I ask the Congress to authorize the detail of American civilian and military personnel to Greece and Turkey, at the request of those countries, to assist in the tasks of reconstruction, and for the purpose of supervising the use of such financial and material assistance as may be furnished. I recommend that authority be provided for the instruction and training of selected Greek and Turkish personnel.

Further, I ask that the Congress provide authority which will permit the speediest and most effective use, in terms of needed commodities, supplies, and equipment, of such funds as may be authorized.

If further funds, or further authority, should be needed for purposes indicated in this message, I shall not hesitate to bring the situation before the Congress. On this subject the Executive and Legislative branches of the Government must work together.

This is a serious course upon which we embark.

I would not recommend it except that the alternative is much more serious.

The United States contributed $341,-000,000,000 toward winning World War II. This is an investment in world freedom and world peace.

The assistance that I am recommending for Greece and Turkey amounts to little more than one tenth of one percent of this investment. It is only common sense that we should safeguard this investment and make sure that it was not in vain.

The seeds of totalitarian regimes are

nurtured by misery and want. They spread and grow in the evil soil of poverty and strife. They reach their full growth when the hope of a people for a better life has died.

We must keep that hope alive.

The free peoples of the world look to us for support in maintaining their freedoms.

If we falter in our leadership, we may endanger the peace of the world — and we shall surely endanger the welfare of our own Nation.

Great responsibilities have been placed upon us by the swift movement of events.

I am confident that the Congress will face these responsibilities squarely.

George C. Marshall: THE MARSHALL PLAN

Secretary of State George C. Marshall opened the way for massive economic aid to Western Europe at a Harvard commencement address on June 5, 1947. Without such aid, he emphasized, political stability could never return to Europe. A rehabilitation of the economic structure of Europe was necessary in order to permit the emergence of political and social conditions in which free institutions could exist. Secretary Marshall's remarks are quoted below in their entirety.

I NEED not tell you gentlemen that the world situation is very serious. That must be apparent to all intelligent people. I think one difficulty is that the problem is one of such enormous complexity that the very mass of facts presented to the public by press and radio make it exceedingly difficult for the man in the street to reach a clear appraisement of the situation. Furthermore, the people of this country are distant from the troubled areas of the earth and it is hard for them to comprehend the plight and consequent reactions of the long-suffering peoples, and the effect of those reactions on their governments in connection with our efforts to promote peace in the world.

In considering the requirements for the rehabilitation of Europe, the physical loss of life, the visible destruction of cities, factories, mines, and railroads was correctly estimated, but it has become obvious during recent months that this visible destruction was probably less serious than the dislocation of the entire fabric of European economy. For the past 10 years conditions have been highly abnormal. The feverish preparation for war and the more feverish maintenance of the war effort engulfed all aspects of national economies. Machinery has fallen into disrepair or is entirely obsolete. Under the arbitrary and destructive Nazi rule, virtually every possible enterprise was geared into the German war machine. Long-standing commercial ties, private institutions, banks, insurance companies, and shipping companies disappeared, through loss of capital, absorption through nationalization, or by simple destruction. In many coun-

From Secretary George C. Marshall's commencement address at Harvard University, June 5, 1947. Department of State *Bulletin*, XVI (June 15, 1947), pp. 1159–1160.

tries, confidence in the local currency has been severely shaken. The breakdown of the business structure of Europe during the war was complete. Recovery has been seriously retarded by the fact that two years after the close of hostilities a peace settlement with Germany and Austria has not been agreed upon. But even given a more prompt solution of these difficult problems, the rehabilitation of the economic structure of Europe quite evidently will require a much longer time and greater effort than had been foreseen.

There is a phase of this matter which is both interesting and serious. The farmer has always produced the foodstuffs to exchange with the city dweller for the other necessities of life. This division of labor is the basis of modern civilization. At the present time it is threatened with breakdown. The town and city industries are not producing adequate goods to exchange with the food-producing farmer. Raw materials and fuel are in short supply. Machinery is lacking or worn out. The farmer or the peasant cannot find the goods for sale which he desires to purchase. So the sale of his farm produce for money which he cannot use seems to him an unprofitable transaction. He, therefore, has withdrawn many fields from crop cultivation and is using them for grazing. He feeds more grain to stock and finds for himself and his family an ample supply of food, however short he may be on clothing and the other ordinary gadgets of civilization. Meanwhile people in the cities are short of food and fuel. So the governments are forced to use their foreign money and credits to procure these necessities abroad. This process exhausts funds which are urgently needed for reconstruction. Thus a very serious situation is rapidly developing which bodes no good for the world. The modern sys-

tem of the division of labor upon which the exchange of products is based is in danger of breaking down.

The truth of the matter is that Europe's requirements for the next three or four years of foreign food and other essential products — principally from America — are so much greater than her present ability to pay that she must have substantial additional help or face economic, social, and political deterioration of a very grave character.

The remedy lies in breaking the vicious circle and restoring the confidence of the European people in the economic future of their own countries and of Europe as a whole. The manufacturer and the farmer throughout wide areas must be able and willing to exchange their products for currencies the continuing value of which is not open to question.

Aside from the demoralizing effect on the world at large and the possibilities of disturbances arising as a result of the desperation of the people concerned, the consequences to the economy of the United States should be apparent to all. It is logical that the United States should do whatever it is able to do to assist in the return of normal economic health in the world, without which there can be no political stability and no assured peace. Our policy is directed not against any country or doctrine but against hunger, poverty, desperation, and chaos. Its purpose should be the revival of a working economy in the world so as to permit the emergence of political and social conditions in which free institutions can exist. Such assistance, I am convinced, must not be on a piecemeal basis as various crises develop. Any assistance that this Government may render in the future should provide a cure rather than a mere palliative. Any government that is willing to assist in the task of recovery will find full cooperation, I am sure, on the part of the United States Government. Any government which maneuvers to block the recovery of other countries cannot expect help from us. Furthermore, government, political parties, or groups which seek to perpetuate human misery in order to profit therefrom politically or otherwise will encounter the opposition of the United States.

It is already evident that, before the United States Government can proceed much further in its efforts to alleviate the situation and help start the European world on its way to recovery, there must be some agreement among the countries of Europe as to the requirements of the situation and the part those countries themselves will take in order to give proper effect to whatever action might be undertaken by this Government. It would be neither fitting nor efficacious for this Government to undertake to draw up unilaterally a program designed

to place Europe on its feet economically. This is the business of the Europeans. The initiative, I think, must come from Europe. The role of this country should consist of friendly aid in the drafting of a European program and of later support of such a program so far as it may be practical for us to do so. The program should be a joint one, agreed to by a number, if not all, European nations.

An essential part of any successful action on the part of the United States is an understanding on the part of the people of America of the character of the problem and the remedies to be applied. Political passion and prejudice should have no part. With foresight, and a willingness on the part of our people to face up to the vast responsibility which history has clearly placed upon our country, the difficulties I have outlined can and will be overcome.

THE BRUSSELS PACT

In confronting Communist expansionism, it was important for the United States and its allies to operate within the confines of the United Nations Charter. Article 51 proclaimed "the . . . right of individual or collective self-defense." Articles 52 and 53 granted recognition to "regional arrangements" provided that such arrangements or agencies and their activities are consistent "with the Purposes and Principles of the United Nations." Thus when Czechoslovakia fell in February, 1948, five nations of Europe banded together in the Brussels Treaty against the threat of Communist subversion, they did so in the name of collective self-defense "in accordance with the Charter of the United Nations."

ARTICLE I

CONVINCED of the close community of their interests and of the necessity of uniting in order to promote the economic recovery of Europe, the High Contracting Parties will so organize and co-

Treaty of Economic, Social and Cultural Collaboration and Collective Self-Defense between the Governments of the United Kingdom and Northern Ireland, Belgium, France, Luxembourg, and the Netherlands, signed at Brussels, March 17, 1948. Extracted from Department of State Publication 5669 (November 1954), pp. 59–62.

ordinate their economic activities as to produce the best possible results, by the elimination of conflict in their economic policies, the co-ordination of production and the development of commercial exchanges.

The co-operation provided for in the preceding paragraph, which will be effected through the Consultative Council referred to in Article VII as well as through other bodies, shall not involve any duplication of, or prejudice to, the work of other economic organizations in which the High Contracting Parties are or may be represented but shall on the contrary assist the work of those organizations.

ARTICLE II

The High Contracting Parties will make every effort in common, both by direct consultation and in specialized agencies, to promote the attainment of a higher standard of living by their peoples and to develop on corresponding lines the social and other related services of their countries.

The High Contracting Parties will consult with the object of achieving the earliest possible application of recommendations of immediate practical interest, relating to social matters, adopted with their approval in the specialized agencies.

They will endeavor to conclude as soon as possible conventions with each other in the sphere of social security.

ARTICLE III

The High Contracting Parties will make every effort in common to lead their peoples towards a better understanding of the principles which form the basis of their common civilization and to promote cultural exchanges by conventions between themselves or by other means.

ARTICLE IV

If any of the High Contracting Parties should be the object of an armed attack in Europe, the other High Contracting Parties will, in accordance with the provisions of Article 51 of the Charter of the United Nations, afford the party so attacked all the military and other aid and assistance in their power.

ARTICLE V

All measures taken as a result of the preceding Article shall be immediately reported to the Security Council. They shall be terminated as soon as the Security Council has taken the measures necessary to maintain or restore international peace and security.

The present Treaty does not prejudice in any way the obligations of the High Contracting Parties under the provisions of the Charter of the United Nations. It shall not be interpreted as affecting in any way the authority and responsibility of the Security Council under the Charter to take at any time such action as it deems necessary in order to maintain or restore international peace and security.

ARTICLE VI

The High Contracting Parties declare, each so far as he is concerned, that none of the international engagements now in force between him and any other of the High Contracting Parties or any third State is in conflict with the provisions of the present Treaty.

None of the High Contracting Parties will conclude any alliance or participate in any coalition directed against any other of the High Contracting Parties.

ARTICLE VII

For the purpose of consulting together on all the questions dealt with in the present Treaty, the High Contracting

Parties will create a Consultative Council, which shall be so organized as to be able to exercise its functions continuously. The Council shall meet at such times as it shall deem fit.

At the request of any of the High Contracting Parties, the Council shall be immediately convened in order to permit the High Contracting Parties to consult with regard to any situation which may constitute a threat to peace, in whatever area this threat should arise; with regard to the attitude to be adopted and the steps to be taken in case of a renewal by Germany of an aggressive policy; or with regard to any situation constituting a danger to economic stability.

ARTICLE VIII

In pursuance of their determination to settle disputes only by peaceful means, the High Contracting Parties will apply to disputes between themselves the following provisions:

The High Contracting Parties will, while the present Treaty remains in force, settle all disputes falling within the scope of Article 36, paragraph 2, of the Statute of the International Court of Justice by referring them to the Court, subject only, in the case of each of them, to any reservation already made by that Party when accepting this clause for compulsory jurisdiction to the extent that that Party may maintain the reservation.

In addition, the High Contracting Parties will submit to conciliation all disputes outside the scope of Article 36, paragraph 2, of the Statute of the International Court of Justice.

In the case of a mixed dispute involving both questions for which conciliation is appropriate and other questions for which judicial settlement is appropriate, any Party to the dispute shall have the right to insist that the judicial settlement of the legal questions shall precede conciliation.

The preceding provisions of this Article in no way affect the application of relevant provisions or agreements prescribing some other method of pacific settlement.

ARTICLE IX

The High Contracting Parties may, by agreement, invite any other State to accede to the present Treaty on conditions to be agreed between them and the State so invited.

Any State so invited may become a Party to the Treaty by depositing an instrument of accession with the Belgian Government.

The Belgian Government will inform each of the High Contracting Parties of the deposit of each instrument of accession.

ARTICLE X

The present Treaty shall be ratified and the instruments of ratification shall be deposited as soon as possible with the Belgian Government.

It shall enter into force on the date of the deposit of the last instrument of ratification and shall thereafter remain in force for fifty years.

After the expiry of the period of fifty years, each of the High Contracting Parties shall have the right to cease to be a party thereto provided that he shall have previously given one year's notice of denunciation to the Belgian Government.

The Belgian Government shall inform the Governments of the other High Contracting Parties of the deposit of each instrument of ratification and of each notice of denunciation.

In witness whereof, the above-mentioned Plenipotentiaries have signed the present Treaty and have affixed thereto their seals.

Done at Brussels, this seventeenth day of March 1948, in English and French, each text being equally authentic, in a single copy which shall remain deposited in the archives of the Belgian Government and of which certified copies shall be transmitted by that Government to each of the other signatories.

U. S. Senate Committee on Foreign Relations: THE NORTH ATLANTIC TREATY

Inspired by the willingness of the Brussels Pact nations to work together in matters economic, political, and cultural as well as military, the United States Senate in a resolution offered by Senator Arthur H. Vandenberg, a Republican leader and former isolationist, applauded Europe's efforts and sought to bolster them. Senate Resolution 239 of June 11, 1948, implicitly recognized that Europe alone could not provide sufficient security for its people and that the United States would have to associate itself "with such regional and other collective arrangements as are based on continuous and effective self-help and mutual aid." Less than a year later, the United States had worked out the kind of "association" that would best help Europe and itself: a North Atlantic Treaty embracing the original five nations of the Brussels Pact. In this treaty for the first time in one hundred and forty-nine years the United States involved itself in an entangling alliance with a European nation. Of the eleven new allies in 1949, nine were demonstrably "European."

THE Parties to this Treaty reaffirm their faith in the purposes and principles of the Charter of the United Nations and their desire to live in peace with all peoples and all governments.

They are determined to safeguard the freedom, common heritage and civilization of their peoples, founded on the principles of democracy, individual liberty and the rule of law.

They seek to promote stability and well-being in the North Atlantic area.

They are resolved to unite their efforts for collective defense and for the preservation of peace and security.

They therefore agree to this North Atlantic Treaty:

ARTICLE 1

The Parties undertake, as set forth in the Charter of the United Nations, to settle any international disputes in which they may be involved by peaceful means in such a manner that international peace and security, and justice, are not endangered, and to refrain in their international relations from the threat or use of force in any manner inconsistent with the purposes of the United Nations.

The full text of The North Atlantic Treaty, signed on April 4, 1949, is in *Hearings*, "North Atlantic Treaty," *U. S. Senate Committee on Foreign Relations, 1st session*, Part I (Washington, 1949), pp. 1–3.

ARTICLE 2

The Parties will contribute toward the further development of peaceful and friendly international relations by strengthening their free institutions, by bringing about a better understanding of the principles upon which these institutions are founded, and by promoting conditions of stability and well-being. They will seek to eliminate conflict in their international economic policies and will encourage economic collaboration between any or all of them.

ARTICLE 3

In order more effectively to achieve the objectives of this Treaty, the Parties, separately and jointly, by means of continuous and effective self-help and mutual aid, will maintain and develop their individual and collective capacity to resist armed attack.

ARTICLE 4

The Parties will consult together whenever, in the opinion of any of them, the territorial integrity, political independence or security of any of the Parties is threatened.

ARTICLE 5

The Parties agree that an armed attack against one or more of them in Europe or North America shall be considered an attack against them all; and consequently they agree that, if such an armed attack occurs, each of them, in exercise of the right of individual or collective self-defense recognized by Article 51 of the Charter of the United Nations, will assist the Party or Parties so attacked by taking forthwith, individually and in concert with the other Parties, such action as it deems necessary, including the use of armed force, to restore and maintain the security of the North Atlantic area.

Any such armed attack and all measures taken as a result thereof shall immediately be reported to the Security Council. Such measures shall be terminated when the Security Council has taken the measures necessary to restore and maintain international peace and security.

ARTICLE 6

For the purpose of Article 5 an armed attack on one or more of the Parties is deemed to include an armed attack on the territory of any of the Parties in Europe or North America, on the Algerian department of France, on the occupation forces of any Party in Europe, on the islands under the jurisdiction of any Party in the North Atlantic area north of the Tropic of Cancer or on the vessels or aircraft in this area of any of the Parties.

ARTICLE 7

This Treaty does not affect, and shall not be interpreted as affecting, in any way the rights and obligations under the Charter of the Parties which are members of the United Nations, or the primary responsibility of the Security Council for the maintenance of international peace and security.

ARTICLE 8

Each Party declares that none of the international engagements now in force between it and any other of the Parties or any third state is in conflict with the provisions of this Treaty, and undertakes not to enter into any international engagement in conflict with this Treaty.

ARTICLE 9

The Parties hereby establish a council, on which each of them shall be represented, to consider matters concerning the implementation of this Treaty. The council shall be so organized as to be able to meet promptly at any time. The council shall set up such subsidiary bodies as may be necessary; in particular it shall establish immediately a defense committee which shall recommend measures for the implementation of Articles 3 and 5.

ARTICLE 10

The Parties may, by unanimous agreement, invite any other European state in a position to further the principles of this Treaty and to contribute to the security of the North Atlantic area to accede to this Treaty. Any state so invited may become a party to the Treaty by depositing its instrument of accession with the Government of the United States of America. The Government of the United States of America will inform each of the Parties of the deposit of each such instrument of accession.

ARTICLE 11

This Treaty shall be ratified and its provisions carried out by the Parties in accordance with their respective constitutional processes. The instruments of ratification shall be deposited as soon as possible with the Government of the United States of America, which will notify all the other signatories of each deposit. The Treaty shall enter into force between the states which have ratified it as soon as the ratifications of the majority of the signatories, including the ratifications of Belgium, Canada, France, Luxembourg, the Netherlands, the United Kingdom and the United States, have

been deposited and shall come into effect with respect to other states on the date of the deposit of their ratifications.

ARTICLE 12

After the Treaty has been in force for ten years, or at any time thereafter, the Parties shall, if any of them so requests, consult together for the purpose of reviewing the Treaty, having regard for the factors then affecting peace and security in the North Atlantic area, including the development of universal as well as regional arrangements under the Charter of the United Nations for the maintenance of international peace and security.

ARTICLE 13

After the Treaty has been in force for twenty years, any Party may cease to be a party one year after its notice of denunciation has been given to the Government of the United States of America, which will inform the Governments of the other Parties of the deposit of each notice of denunciation.

ARTICLE 14

This Treaty, of which the English and French texts are equally authentic, shall be deposited in the archives of the Government of the United States of America. Duly certified copies thereof will be transmitted by that Government to the Governments of the other signatories.

In witness whereof, the undersigned plenipotentiaries have signed this Treaty.

Done at Washington, the fourth day of April, 1949.

II. DEBATE OVER THE TREATY—1949

Department of State: THE ATLANTIC PACT AND
UNITED STATES POLICIES

*In preparation for debate in the Senate, the Administration empha-
sized in a State Department pamphlet the indivisibility of European
and American security. The Treaty was to be regarded as fully in
accord with other American measures to support peace since 1945.*

PRESIDENT TRUMAN'S "POINT THREE"

PRESIDENT Truman's Inaugural
Address was both a statement of
American principles and a program of
action, a reaffirmation of the policies
which have guided the United States in
world affairs and a selection of the
means to be used to make these policies
most effective. The four major courses
of action he announced are dependent
one upon the other and all of them depend upon the day-to-day execution of
the whole body of United States foreign
policy which expresses the character, the
way of life, and the intent of the American people. The principles which have
led to the great actions of the United
States in the past are those which now
give power and moral substance to the
cooperation the United States looks forward to establishing with the other countries of the North Atlantic area. The
people of the United States, the President declared:

. . . believe that all men have a right to
equal justice under law and equal opportunity to share in the common good. We believe that all men have the right to freedom
of thought and expression. . . .

The American people desire, and are determined to work for, a world in which all
nations and all peoples are free to govern
themselves as they see fit and to achieve a
decent and satisfying life. Above all else, our
people desire, and are determined to work
for, peace on earth — a just and lasting peace
— based on genuine agreement freely arrived
at by equals.

The third of the four major courses of
United States action outlined by President Truman was directed squarely at
a peace "based on genuine agreement
freely arrived at by equals." Principle
and method were tied clearly together.

. . . we will strengthen freedom-loving nations against the dangers of aggression.

We are now working out with a number
of countries a joint agreement designed to
strengthen the security of the North Atlantic
area. Such an arrangement would take the
form of a collective defense arrangement
within the terms of the United Nations
Charter.

We have already established such a defense pact for the Western Hemisphere by
the treaty of Rio de Janeiro.

The primary purpose of these agreements
is to provide unmistakable proof of the joint
determination of the free countries to resist
armed attack from any quarter. Each country participating in these arrangements must
contribute all it can to the common defense.

If we can make it sufficiently clear, in ad-

From "The North Atlantic Treaty," Department of State *Publication,* no. 3462 (March, 1949),
pp. 8–12.

vance, that any armed attack affecting our national security would be met with overwhelming force, the armed attack might never occur.

COOPERATION FOR WORLD PEACE

The United States has vigorously supported the United Nations and the related agencies. In his Inaugural Address President Truman stated again the determination of the United States to continue to search for ways to strengthen their authority and increase their effectiveness. This determination has led and will continue to lead to practical action — aid to the war devastated areas, aid to Greece and Turkey, the effort to secure agreement on the international control of atomic energy, the European Recovery Program, cooperation in establishing the Organization of American States, the proposal for a cooperative world program of technical assistance, and the joint action in protecting the security of the North Atlantic area. These actions are based on the assumption that each Member of the United Nations is obligated to observe in all of its relations with other countries the principles it pledged itself to support when it signed the Charter.

SECURITY ARRANGEMENTS

United States policy recognizes that the United Nations is not yet the perfected instrument of world security. The United Nations was founded on the premise of Great Power cooperation. Its structure is therefore such that, if any one Great Power is unwilling to cooperate, it can seriously impede efforts for peace within the organization. Soviet obstruction in the United Nations, with excessive use of the veto, and Soviet failure to live up to its obligations under the Charter have prompted Members

which are active in support of the purposes and principles of the Charter to take steps to assure the freedom and independence of certain Members of the United Nations. The United States has taken part in some of these actions and has given support, both moral and material, to others. President Truman's message to Congress on March 17, 1948, referred specifically to the Brussels Pact:

. . . This development deserves our full support. I am confident that the United States will, by appropriate means, extend to the free nations the support which the situation requires. I am sure that the determination of the free countries of Europe to protect themselves will be matched by an equal determination on our part to help them to do so.

This policy of support was given a broader context three months later when on June 11, 1948, the United States Senate, by an overwhelming vote, recommended:

Progressive development of regional and other collective arrangements for individual and collective self-defense in accordance with the purposes, principles, and provisions of the Charter.

Association of the United States, by constitutional process, with such regional and other collective arrangements as are based on continuous and effective self-help and mutual aid, and as affect its national security.

Contributing to the maintenance of peace by making clear its determination to exercise the right of individual or collective self-defense under article 51 should any armed attack occur affecting its national security.

World Wars I and II demonstrate that the security of the United States is directly related to the security of Western Europe and that the nations on both sides of the North Atlantic are bound together by a natural community of interests. The Atlantic Pact is a formal acknowledgment of this relationship and reflects their conviction that an armed attack can be prevented only by making clear in advance their determination collectively to resist such an attack if it should occur. Such a collective security arrangement is necessary, in the view of the United States, to protect the North Atlantic community and its own security.

By enabling its members to confront a potential aggressor with preponderant power — military, economic, and spiritual — the Atlantic Pact will help to restore the confidence and sense of security which are essential for full economic and political stability. Its political, psychological and military values are each important and, in fact, inseparable. By reducing the chances of war, by increasing confidence and stability, and by providing the basis for effective collective defense should it be necessary, the Pact can aid materially in establishing in Western Europe the atmosphere necessary for economic recovery and bring closer the fuller life which is possible in a cooperative world society adjusted to the peaceful uses of modern scientific and technical advances.

The ability of freedom-loving peoples to preserve their independence, in the face of totalitarian threats, depends upon their determination to do so. That determination, in turn, depends upon the de-velopment of healthy political and economic life and a genuine sense of security. A belief in this power of self-determination led the United States to embark upon a policy of assisting Greece and Turkey through the Greek and Turkish Aid Program, and later, the European countries through the European Recovery Program. The United States is now contemplating entry into the North Atlantic Pact as a means of giving effective support in the area of collective security to the purposes and principles of the United Nations as set forth in the Charter. If the American people approve this step, the government's objective will be the same as the one on which United States policies now converge, the restoration to international society of the conditions essential to the effective operation of the machinery of the United Nations and the progressive attainment of the objectives stated in the United Nations Charter. In the words of President Truman:

We are moving on with other nations to build an even stronger structure of international order and justice. We shall have as our partners countries which, no longer solely concerned with the problem of national survival, are now working to improve the standards of living of all their people.

Slowly but surely we are weaving a world fabric of international security and growing prosperity.

Robert A. Taft: A CONSERVATIVE OPPOSES THE TREATY

Senator Robert A. Taft of Ohio was the most influential Republican in the Congress between 1946 and his death in 1953. An isolationist who deplored the label, Senator Taft opposed the Treaty as a dangerous deviation from past policies. While conceding the dangers confronting Europe, he suggested that better means might have been found to cope with them: the restructuring of the United Nations or a unilateral extension of the Monroe Doctrine to Europe. Instead, the United States chose the path of alliance which put the United States "at the mercy of the foreign policies of 11 other nations . . . for a period of 20 years."

LET us begin to make our own foreign policy, instead of letting Moscow make it for us. Let us begin to carry out our own American world revolution, for greater abundance and greater freedom for all mankind, using the tools and the ideas and the principles with which we have been so successful at home to create a similar free and abundant world abroad. [Applause.]

Mr. Taft obtained the floor. . . .

Mr. Taft. Mr. President, I listened with great interest to the speech made today by the distinguished Senator from Iowa [*Mr. Gillette*]. I wish to assure the Senate that I have not consulted with the Senator from Iowa; but the arguments I shall make against the Atlantic Pact are very similar to the ones he made, and I agree thoroughly with the very effective argument and very effective speech he made on that subject. However, the same arguments have led me to the conclusion that I must vote against the pact, rather than for it, as he has announced he intends to do.

It is with great regret that I have come to my conclusion, but I have come to it because I think the pact carries with it an obligation to assist in arming, at our expense, the nations of Western Europe, because with that obligation I believe it will promote war in the world rather than peace, and because I think that with the arms plan it is wholly contrary to the spirit of the obligations we assumed in the United Nations Charter. I would vote for the pact if a reservation were adopted denying any legal or moral obligation to provide arms.

The purpose of American foreign policy, as I see it, is to maintain the freedom of the people of this country and, insofar as consistent with that purpose, to keep this country at peace. We are, of course, interested in the welfare of the rest of the world because we are a humane nation. Our huge economic aid, however, is based on the belief that a world which is prosperous and well off is less likely to engage in war than one in which there are great inequities in the economic condition of different people.

In the past, we have considered that the best method of preserving the peace and security of this country is the maintenance of American armed forces sufficient to defend us against attack, and a wise diplomatic policy which does not antagonize other nations. Those still are

From Robert A. Taft, speech delivered on July 11, 1949, *Congressional Record, U. S. Senate, 81st Congress, 1st Session* (Washington: U. S. Government Printing Office, 1949), pp. 9205–9206.

the main essentials to the maintenance of peace in the world of today.

But as the world shrinks in size, as new weapons are developed, as we inevitably become more involved in the affairs of other countries, it has become apparent that these weapons alone will not assure peace. And so we have committed ourselves to the principle of an association of sovereign nations banded together to preserve peace by preventing and punishing aggression. In the United Nations Charter we accepted the principle that we would go to war in association with other nations against a nation found by the Security Council to be an aggressor. That was a tremendous departure from our previous policy, but one which I have always urged and approved from the days of the League of Nations. I believe that all nations must ultimately agree, if we are to have peace, to an international law defining the duties and obligations of such nations, particularly with reference to restraint from aggression and war. I believe that there should be international courts to determine whether nations are abiding by that law, and I believe that there should be a joint armed force to enforce that law and the decisions of that court. I believe that in the end, the public opinion of the world will come to support the principle that nations like individuals are bound by law, and will insist that any nation which violates the law be promptly subjected to the joint action of nations guided by a determination to enforce the laws of peace.

It is quite true that the United Nations Charter as drafted does not as yet reach the ideals of international peace and justice which I have described, but it goes a long way in that direction. It is defective principally because any one of the large nations can veto the action of the Security Council, and because there is not sufficient emphasis on law and justice as a guide to the action of the Security Council. But we have advised the President that prompt action should be taken to improve the Charter. Senate Resolution No. 239, adopted by the Senate on June 11, 1948, contained three clauses proposing improvement in the United Nations Charter: First, a voluntary agreement to remove the veto from many questions; second, maximum efforts to obtain agreement for a United Nations armed force and the reduction of national armaments; and third, a review of the Charter by a general conference called under article 109 of the Charter. As far as I know, the State Department has disregarded these injunctions of Senate Resolution 239 and concentrated only on that clause of the resolution which proposed a compact under article 51, based on the defects of the United Nations Charter.

The distinguished Senator from Michigan has called the attention of the Senator from Iowa [*Mr. Gillette*] to the fact that the State Department has urged these changes on the United Nations. I can only say that both the Senator from Iowa and myself do follow the newspapers, and that if they have so urged, no emphasis has been placed upon the matter. There has been no effort to stir up public opinion in favor of such changes, as there has been in favor of the Atlantic Pact. So far as I know, no suggestion whatever has been made that any conference be called under article 109 of the Charter, which I think would be the only effective means of securing improvements in the Charter.

The North Atlantic Treaty might have been so drafted as to create a small United Nations within the larger group, improving upon the United Nations Charter, eliminating its defects, and furnishing an example of an improved international organization which could be followed by the United Nations itself. It might have established a law between the nations signing it and a force to prevent aggression between those nations without veto and with reliance on the decision of a competent court to administer justice. This was suggested by Mr. Hamilton Fish Armstrong in an article in *Foreign Affairs* in October 1948. It is the general plan suggested in Senate Resolution 133, introduced by the distinguished junior Senator from Alabama and 10 other Senators on Friday of last week, with which I have great sympathy.

But the State Department did not adopt any of these suggestions and has shown no intention of doing so. We have to consider here the North Atlantic Treaty as it has been drafted, without the improvements Senators would like to see made, but which 12 nations probably would not agree to once this treaty is ratified. We abandoned the chance of getting those when we signed the treaty in its present form. The Atlantic Treaty as drawn is certainly no improvement over the United Nations, nor can it by any stretch of the imagination be regarded as a perfection of or supplement to that Charter. From the point of view of an international organization, it is a step backward. Apart from the obligation to provide arms, the treaty is permitted by the Charter, which says:

Nothing in the present Charter shall impair the inherent right of individual or collective self-defense if an armed attack occurs against a member of the United Nations until the Security Council has taken the measures necessary to maintain international peace and security.

The Charter merely recognizes this inherent right as necessary because the veto provision of the Charter may result in complete inaction on the part of the Security Council. But certainly in all other respects the treaty far more resembles a military alliance than it does any international association of nations. As the Senator from Iowa so forcefully said, it is a step backward in the progress toward international peace and justice.

What is the nature of that treaty?

It is obviously, and I do not think it can be questioned, a defensive military alliance between certain nations, the essence of which is an obligation under article 5 to go to war if necessary with any nation which attacks any one of the signers of the treaty. Such an attack may come from outsiders or it may come from one of the signers of the treaty itself. The obligation is completely binding for a period of 20 years. It imposes an obligation upon the United States to each member nation whether or not there is consultation or joint action by the Council, or a finding by any court that an unjustified armed attack has occurred. Our obligation is self-executing upon the occurrence of an armed attack.

Some doubt will always remain as to whether the Congress must declare war before our armed forces actually take part. I am inclined to think such action is not necessary if the President chooses to use our armed forces when an ally is attacked. But whether it is or not, the obligation to go to war seems to me binding upon the United States as a nation, so that Congress would be obligated to declare war if that were necessary to comply with the provisions of the treaty. It is pointed out that the President could fail to act and Congress could refuse to declare war, but certainly we are not making a treaty on the theory that we expect to violate it in accordance with our own sweet will.

It is correctly pointed out that the exact measures which we are obligated to take will be determined by us, and that it may not be necessary to go to the extent of a declaration of war. We do reserve certain discretion, but as I see it, we do not reserve any discretion on the question, for instance, whether the armed attack is justified, as a reason for supporting it. If one of the members of the pact provides an attack, even by conduct which we disapprove, we would still apparently be bound to go to its defense. By executing a treaty of this kind, we put ourselves at the mercy of the foreign policies of 11 other nations, and do so for a period of 20 years. The Charter is obviously aimed at possible Russian aggression against Western Europe, but the obligation assumed is far broader than that. I emphasize again that the obligation is much more unconditional, much less dependent on legal processes and much less dependent on joint action than the obligation of the United Nations Charter.

And yet in spite of these dangers, I have wanted to vote in favor of the Atlantic Pact for one reason and would still do so if the question of arms were not involved. I fully agree with the effective argument in favor of the pact made by the distinguished Senator from Michigan because of its warning to the USSR. I think we should make it clear to the USSR that if it attacks Western Europe, it will be at war with us. I fully agree with the statement of the disinguished Senator from Michigan:

It is not the military forces in being which measure the impact of this knock-out admonition. Its invincible power for peace is the awesome fact that any aggressor upon the North Atlantic community knows in advance from the very moment he launches his conquest, he will forthwith face whatever cumulative opposition these united allies in their own wisdom deem necessary to beat him to his knees and to restore peace and security. It is this total concept which, in my view, would give even a reincarnated Hitler pause.

I agree that if the Kaiser had known that England and the United States would be in the war, the First World War might never have begun. I agree that if Hitler had known the United States would be in the war, the Second World War might not have begun. I favor the extension of the Monroe Doctrine under present circumstances to Western Europe.

It is said that the Atlantic Treaty is simply another Monroe Doctrine. I wish it were. That would be much more acceptable to me than the Atlantic pact, arms or no arms. Let me point out the vital differences. The Monroe Doctrine was a unilateral declaration. We were free to modify it or withdraw from it at any moment. This treaty, adopted to deal with a particular emergency today, is binding upon us for 20 years to cover all kinds of circumstances which cannot possibly be foreseen. The Monroe Doctrine left us free to determine the merits of each dispute which might arise and to judge the justice and the wisdom of war in the light of the circumstances at the time. The present treaty obligates us to go to war if certain facts occur. The Monroe Doctrine imposed no obligation whatever to assist any American Nation by giving it arms or even economic aid. We were free to fight the war in such a manner as we might determine, or not at all. This treaty imposes on us a continuous obligation for 20 years to give aid to all the other members of the pact, and, I believe, to give military aid to all the other members of the pact.

All kinds of circumstances may arise which will make our obligation most inconvenient. The government of one of these nations may be taken over by the Communist Party of that nation. The distinguished Senator from Michigan says that we are then released from our obligation, but I see no basis whatever for such a conclusion. If that were true of a Communist government, it might also be true of a Socialist government if we did not happen to approve of socialism at the time. Presumably, it could be true of a Fascist government, one similar, perhaps, to that existing in Spain which has been denounced recently by the Secretary of State, and which is not very different from the dictatorship of Portugal, which is a member of the pact and which has not a truly democratic form of government.

I cannot find anything in this treaty which releases us because we do not happen to like the officials in charge of the member nations at the particular moment.

Obviously, any help we give one of these nations today may be used later for aggressive purposes, against Russia or its satellites, or neutrals, or members of the pact, or it may even be used against us when we try to fulfill our obligation to other members of the pact. Except for the warning conveyed to Soviet Russia, this treaty does not bear the slightest resemblance to the Monroe Doctrine.

It is said that the treaty is in strict accordance with Senate Resolution 239 adopted by the Senate in June 1948. I did not vote upon that resolution, but I believe this treaty goes far beyond the advice there given by the Senate. That resolution approved the general theory

of a treaty to exercise the right of individual or collective self-defense in case of an armed attack in accordance with the purposes, principles, and provisions of the Charter, but I do not think it suggested the providing of arms to members of the pact, or even the obligations of article 5. Paragraph 4 of the resolution, which is the closest one to authorizing the present treaty, sounds more like a new Monroe Doctrine than it does like a treaty. It does not refer to a treaty of any kind. It says that one of our objectives should be contributing to the maintenance of peace by making clear our determination to exercise the right of individual or collective self-defense under article 51 should any armed attack occur affecting our national security. This looks far more like a warning to Russia than it does like a defensive military alliance of the present type. The distinguished Senator from Michigan, in explaining the resolution at that time, said:

It declines automatically military alliances. It declines all peacetime renewals of the old, open-ended lend-lease formula. It declines unilateral responsibility for the fate of Western Europe. It is none of those things. It is the exact opposite.

The present treaty is a military alliance. The present treaty does contemplate a peacetime renewal of the old, open-ended, lend-lease formula. The present treaty assumes unilateral responsibility for the fate of Western Europe. We are obligated to go to the defense of any nation whether the other members of the pact do so or not, or whatever their consultation may advise.

Henry A. Wallace: A LIBERAL TESTIFIES AGAINST THE TREATY

Henry A. Wallace, Secretary of Agriculture and Vice-President under Roosevelt and Secretary of Commerce under Truman, had broken with the Administration over foreign policy in 1946 and had run for President as the Progressive Party candidate in 1948. He accused the Administration of an undeclared war against Russia and of refusing to accept Russian offers of peace talks. The military alliance of the Atlantic Pact would only harden the difference between the two countries as well as drain American resources and undermine the credibility of the United Nations.

STATEMENT OF HON. HENRY A. WALLACE, REPRESENTING THE PROGRESSIVE PARTY OF AMERICA

MR. WALLACE. Two years ago when President Truman announced the Truman doctrine of containing Russia and communism at every point I predicted it would cause us to bleed from every pore. I said that it was a vain and hopeless policy to contain an idea with guns; that the cost would be fantastically high, that it could have no end but war.

DANGERS OF THE NORTH ATLANTIC TREATY

The North Atlantic Military Pact is now taking us toward that end. It would make all Europe into a Greece, and perhaps a China. It demands spending by Americans without limit in dollars or time. It will create an intolerable burden on our own people, exacting lower living standards and the loss of fundamental freedoms.

The pact destroys the chances of European recovery. A permanently militarized Europe is doomed to living on an American dole. And it will accelerate all those social strains and increase that poverty which are the breeding ground for the very doctrine that it would contain. The pact is not an instru-

ment of defense but a military alliance designed for aggression. It bypasses the United Nations and violates its Charter in a most flagrant manner. It takes away from Congress the power to declare war and lodges it in the hands of a military staff 3,000 miles from the seat of our Government. It becomes the instrument for intervention in the internal affairs of Europe. It divides the world permanently into two armed camps. And it provocatively establishes military bases on the borders of the Soviet Union.

DOCTRINE OF CONTAINMENT

I am confident that if we examine the maze of contradictions and difficulties into which the pact leads us, we shall reject it, as well as the arms program with which it is linked, and the doctrine of containment on which both rest. That doctrine is not an American doctrine, but a policy first advocated and since pursued by Mr. Churchill. It has failed ever since Mr. Churchill failed to "strangle bolshevism," as he puts it, in 1919. With but a short interlude during the war, Mr. Churchill has steadily adhered

From Henry A. Wallace, "North Atlantic Treaty," *Hearings, U. S. Senate Committee on Foreign Relations, 81st Congress, 1st Session.* (Washington: U. S. Government Printing Office, 1949), pp. 417–421, 431–432.

to a doctrine which can serve only the domestic purposes of reaction and the narrow interests of a decaying imperialism.

It is not the business of an American, in or out of the Senate or executive branches of Government, to further the policies of Mr. Churchill — and the small group of military men and imperialists who join him.

It is the business of an American to look after our own national interest. For more than three years now, we have been wasting our resources in furthering the narrow interests represented by Mr. Churchill. The end of that policy can only be a war from which we have nothing to gain even should we be fortunate enough to win a military victory.

There will be only the loss of trillions of dollars and untold millions of American lives, and, in all likelihood, the end of our system of government.

It is the plain duty of every American to stop and reconsider this policy which will bankrupt our people, create intolerable burdens on both America and Europe, and can have no end but war. I assert that that policy has been a failure in any realistic sense during the past three years, a failure that is spelled out for us every day in the headlines from China. It is written into our tax payments. It is apparent in the bogging down in this Congress of the promised program of domestic reform, and in the lengthening lines of the unemployed.

I say that the time has come to substitute for the war policy a peace policy which will restore the basis of great-power unity within the United Nations and build a productive world.

INCOMPATIBILITY WITH UNITED NATIONS

I ask this committee — in this spirit — to examine with me the pact and the testimony which has been presented to you in its support.

In his appearance before your committee, Secretary of State Acheson said: "The hopes of the American people for peace with freedom and justice are based on the United Nations." To this statement I most heartily subscribe.

But when Mr. Acheson claims that the pact "is an essential instrument for strengthening the United Nations," he is being far less than frank with the American people.

For the plain fact is that the pact substitutes for the one world of the United Nations the two hostile worlds of a "divided nation." Moreover, it flagrantly violates the plain provisions of the Charter itself.

The United Nations as envisioned by Franklin Roosevelt arose from the determination of the war-weary peoples to abandon power blocs and military alliances for a world organization based on the agreement of the great powers to work together as sovereign and equal nations for the maintenance of world peace.

Secretary of State Stettinius, appearing before this committee just four years ago, made our choice clear. He told you that there were two postwar roads open to the United States — one the road of great-power alliances, the other the road of collective security through the United Nations.

He made it clear that the United States was rejecting the first road because it was alien to our traditions, because it was warlike, and because it could not secure the peace.

He said:

We know that for the United States — and for other great powers — there can be no humanly devised methods of defining precisely the geographic areas in which their security interests begin or cease to exist. We realize, in short, that each is a world-wide problem and that the maintenance of peace, and not merely its restoration, depends primarily upon the unity of the great powers.

There were theoretically two alternative means of preserving this unity —

said Secretary Stettinius.

The first was through the formation of a permanent alliance among the great powers. This method might have been justified on narrow, strategic grounds, but it would have been repugnant to our traditional policy. It also would have contained elements of danger because it might have been interpreted as a menace by nations not party to it. Accordingly, this method was rejected.

The second method was through the establishment of a general security system based upon the principle of sovereign equality of all nations. The provisions for the Security Council recognize the special responsibilities of the great powers for maintaining the peace and the fact that the maintenance of their unity is the crucial political problem of our time.

This is from the report to the President by Secretary Stettinius on the results of the San Francisco Conference on June 26, 1945, appearing in hearings before the United States Senate Committee on Foreign Relations, Seventy-ninth Congress, first session, July 8, 1946, at page 72.

Yet today, Mr. Acheson presses upon your committee a treaty which embodies the very policy that our Nation rejected four years ago. And he does so in the name of strengthening the United Nations.

The Wall Street Journal, with which I do not often agree, spoke the blunt truth when it said that "propaganda notwithstanding, the Atlantic Pact does nul-

lify the principle of the United Nations" and marks "the triumph of jungle law over international cooperation on a world scale."

The pact not only rejects the basic principles upon which the United Nations was founded. It violates the plain provisions of the Charter.

REGIONALISM AND THE TREATY

Initially an attempt was made to justify the pact as a regional agreement under article 52. That attempt now appears to have been abandoned. The argument that a pact covering all the territory from the Aleutian Islands to the Mediterranean and from North Africa to Scandinavia constitutes a "regional agreement" is too thin even for our State Department. Indeed, the argument now runs the other way. It is now insisted that the pact is not a regional agreement. For the State Department has belatedly recognized that if it were, any enforcement measures would require Security Council authorization under article 53, the very procedure which the authors of the pact want desperately to avoid by bypassing the United Nations entirely.

SELF-DEFENSE AND THE TREATY

The proponents of the pact argue that it is authorized by article 51 of the Charter which preserves the inherent right of individual or collective self-defense "if an armed attack occurs against a member of the United Nations." But this article affords no support for the military alliance contemplated by the pact. It simply preserves the inherent right of every nation to repel invasion. It is not a blind behind which military alliances outside of the United Nations can be freely entered into. No armed attack has "occurred" against which the Charter authorizes measures of self-defense. Article 51 does not permit a group of nations to determine for themselves that there is a potential threat of aggression and to enter into an alliance outside of the United Nations for the purpose of resisting it when it comes. To do so would destroy the supreme power of the Security Council to determine the existence of aggression and threats to peace.

The emergency situation to which article 51 addresses itself is similarly dealt with in section 10 of article 1 of our own Constitution.

This section prohibits the separate States, without the consent of Congress, to make an agreement or compact with another State or engage in war, "unless actually invaded or in such imminent danger as will not admit of delay."

I cannot believe, if the State of Michigan feared a possible attack from Canada — that Senator Vandenberg would argue the constitutional right of his State to enter into a compact with Texas, or Florida, to raise an army, organize a joint military council, and engage in other armed preparations in the name of self-defense. Section 10 of article 1 of our Constitution does not supersede the war and treaty-making powers of the National Government.

No more does article 51 of the Charter supersede the peace-making powers of the Security Council.

Yet that is exactly the interpretation which our State Department would place upon it.

Not only does the pact destroy the basis on which the United Nations was founded and violate its Charter. It would also appear to make impossible a return to the one-world principle. . . .

CONSEQUENCES OF THE ATLANTIC TREATY

As I have pointed out, any fair appraisal of its consequences demonstrates that it can lead only to national insolvency, the surrender of our traditional freedoms, war, a possible military disaster, and the certain sacrifice not only of life and treasure but of the very system of government which it is supposed to preserve.

I say that there is an honorable, a peaceful and a practical alternative to this mad course. I say that great nations which really believe in peace can find the road to peace.

The Russians have shown their willingness to travel that road by lifting the Berlin blockade that seemed to stand across it. If the administration sincerely desires peace, let it state its terms to the Russians. Let the heads of both nations, after preparation at the expert level, sit down to negotiate. Peace will require compromise and accommodation on both sides.

But no government that sincerely wants to serve its people can refuse to discuss the terms of peace and instead engages in war alliances and initiate armaments races.

PRINCIPLES FOR UNITED STATES-SOVIET AGREEMENTS

I present again as a basis for such discussions the major points on which agreement can be reached without sacrifice to any American principle or interest.

First, the conclusion of a treaty that would establish a unified and democratic Germany dedicated to peace and stripped of its war potential.

Second, agreement to refrain from interference in the internal affairs of other nations.

Third, agreement by both nations to give up all military bases in other U.N. countries and to halt the export of weapons to other nations.

Fourth, the resumption of unrestricted trade, the establishment of the free movement of citizens and the resumption of free scientific and cultural exchanges between the two countries.

Fifth, a general reduction of armaments that would free the economies of all the world of the burdensome weight of arms and enable them to devote their energies and resources to peacetime production.

Finally, the establishment of a World Reconstruction and Development Agency within the U.N. to build a productive and economically unified Europe, without barriers between East and West, and to assist the free development of the industrially backward countries of Asia, Latin America, and Africa.

This program is the practical, the sane, the peaceful alternative to the Atlantic Pact.

By withholding action on the pact, it is within the power of your committee to create the atmosphere in which this program can be discussed by the diplomatic representatives of the United States and Russia as they bring the Berlin blockade to an end and prepare to tackle the German problem.

It is a program which can end the cold war and avert the atom war.

It is a program completely in our own national interest that yet serves the best interests of a growing and united world.

We insure our own enduring prosperity by helping other nations to a better life.

It offers security based on friendship, not fear.

It opens up a new century of hope for mankind.

III. INTERPRETATION OF THE TREATY, 1949–1950

Lawrence S. Kaplan: NATO AND THE LANGUAGE OF ISOLATIONISM

In the following article, Lawrence S. Kaplan, Professor of History at Kent State University, shows how the language of isolationism was used by Administration supporters in the Senate to justify the Treaty. Thus, the United States was persuaded to enter NATO with the assumption that the pact confirmed the spirit of the Monroe Doctrine and had nothing in common with the old European military alliance.

"ISOLATIONISM" is a term that has gone out of fashion since World War II. It suggests to most an ostrich-like withdrawal from reality equaled only by the behavior of "one-worlders" but lacking the idealistic strain that is at least accorded the latter. Such major actions as participation in the United Nations, sponsorship of the Marshall Plan, and planning of the North Atlantic Treaty attest to America's acceptance of new responsibilities in world affairs, and with it, the discarding of an old and cherished philosophy. The vast majority of Americans presumably recognize that in the face of the Soviet challenge the isolation of an earlier age has become either a luxury that can no longer be afforded or an embarrassing legacy that must be concealed whenever possible.

Despite measures committing the nation to a course of action that other generations might not have sanctioned, it is worth questioning whether the ideas and ideals of isolationism have been as overwhelmed by recent events as the term itself. The emotions aroused by isolationist slogans and catchwords still play an important role in foreign policy making, to the extent that policies directly opposed to the traditions of the past have to be defended in the name of isolationism. No better example of this assertion is afforded than the language and rationalizations used by the adherents of the North Atlantic Treaty in 1949 to win acceptance of that symbol of America's new role on the world stage.

Isolationism's longevity is deserved; for almost a century it represented concepts that furthered the national interest of a small power in a hostile world. Memories of colonial experiences made it clear to Americans that a close connection with Europe would victimize the United States. The new republic might succumb once again to foreign control; at best, it would become a pawn of larger and stronger countries in their struggle for power. Hence the physical separation created by three thousand miles of water could well be considered as divine consecration of a new and better society than the European system of power politics. On a practical basis, isolationism meant opportunity for devel-

From Lawrence S. Kaplan, "NATO and the Language of Isolationism," *South Atlantic Quarterly,* LVII (April, 1958), pp. 204–216. Reprinted with permission of the Duke University Press.

oping a continent free from European competition, profitable commerce with all nations with no alliances to restrict its scope, and a respect for international law and justice without any commitments to enforce them. Isolationism was a useful aid in the development of nineteenth-century America.

The principal themes of isolation, particularly the benefits of America's remoteness from Europe and the dangers of military alliances, have been hallowed by their incorporation into a few major foreign policy proclamations of the most distinguished Founding Fathers — Washington's Farewell Address, Jefferson's First Inaugural Address, and the Monroe Doctrine.

Although each document dealt with the immediate problems of 1796 or 1801 or 1823, isolated slogans and phrases abstracted from the texts have been elevated by generations of politicians to the plane of mystic revelations on the special destiny of America. Consequently, most questions of foreign policy have come to be measured against the imperatives of Washington's observations on America's differences from Europe, of Jefferson's warnings against entanglement in foreign alliances, and of Monroe's pronouncement on the inviolability of the Western Hemisphere. While the nation changed in size and in power, the catchwords of isolation did not, and isolationism inevitably became little more than congeries of slogans appealing to the emotions and to nostalgia rather than a rational response to the nation's needs, as it had been when the Doctrine was first espoused.

The potency of these talismans of foreign policy was fully apparent to the Truman Administration when it decided that United States participation in a North Atlantic Treaty was necessary to deter further Soviet expansion after World War II. Presumably the simplest method of achieving this end would have been American association with the Western Union (the Brussels Pact organization created in 1948 by Britain, France, the Netherlands, Belgium, and Luxembourg) in such a way that the United States would be unmistakably part of the alliance. The effect of this action would have served unquestionably to strengthen Europe's defense against Communist expansion.

Evidence that the American government was at least responsive to the needs of Western Europe was offered by the impressive support given by the Senate to the Vandenberg Resolution of June, 1948, approving the "association of the United States, by constitutional process, with such regional and other collective arrangements as are based on continuous and effective self-help and mutual aid." The Brussels Pact seemed to fulfill all the requirements suggested by the Resolution: it proclaimed loyalty to the provisions of the United Nations Charter; it was a collective action exemplifying mutual aid; and the security of the United States rested upon the survival of Western Europe. Yet no one could say with assurance that the legislators who voted 64 to 6 for Senate Resolution 239 were prepared to accept its full implications and scrap a one-hundred-and-fifty-year tradition of foreign policy by joining the Western Union.

A solution had to be worked out that would give Europe the sense of security it lacked, would insure European contributions to defense, and would deter Soviet aggression without running afoul of emotions generated by the words of Washington's Farewell Address and the Monroe Doctrine. The answer to this problem lay in the creation of a new and broader pact, the enlarging of the Brussels Treaty to include twelve nations, among which would be Canada, the United States, and Iceland as well as countries of Western Europe. This change would not only obviate the charge that the United States would be joining a "European" alliance but would also provide a more defensible strategic area. Military security would be assured and Communism deterred by the agreement of the members that "an armed attack against one or more of them in Europe or North America shall be considered an attack against them all." On April 4, 1949, the United States signed the North Atlantic Treaty with eleven European and American powers.

The judgment of the leaders of the Truman Administration and of the Senate was vindicated when the treaty was exposed to full public debate. From April 27 intermittently to May 18 the Senate Committee on Foreign Relations listened to ninety-six witnesses discuss the treaty, and of this group fifty opposed it. In clear terms public and private witnesses ranging over the entire ideological spectrum assailed the pact as a violation of American principles of foreign policy.

In observing the method whereby advocates of the treaty in the Senate and in the Administration blunted criticism and set forth the virtues of the new program, one can uncover a pattern of argument revealing how the North Atlantic Treaty fitted into the isolationist tradition. Instead of avoiding such subjects as Washington's Farewell Address, Jefferson's First Inaugural, and the Monroe Doctrine as a source of potential embarrassment, the treaty's managers appear to have gone out of their way in their testimony and in leading questions posed to witnesses to show that the treaty con-

formed not only with the spirit but also with the letter of isolationism. Anticipating the strategy of their opponents, they put the emotionally charged words of Washington, Jefferson, and Monroe to the service of a new American foreign policy, thereby upsetting those critics who would have used the same language to damn the treaty.

The first, and in many ways the most powerful, element of isolationism was the projection of the physical separation of Europe from America to a psychological plane through images inspired by such proclamations as the Monroe Doctrine. On the surface it seemed virtually impossible to reconcile a doctrine resting on an eternal cleavage between the Old World and the New with a doctrine that would tie them together again.

The foes of the North Atlantic Treaty were not slow in pointing out the discrepancies between the nature and purposes of the Monroe Doctrine and those of the treaty. An obvious stumbling block was the fact that the countries with which the United States proposed to associate were for the most part the very ones against which the Monroe Doctrine had been directed. Lest their evil deeds be forgotten, one particularly vehement witness felt it necessary to remind the Senators that one has only to look at the map of Latin America today to find evidence of territories seized by England, France, and the Netherlands before the Monroe Doctrine went into effect. The implication was that these countries would now use the Atlantic Pact to win American support for new depredations. The United States would then be on the side of those who would destroy the Monroe Doctrine, and the stigma of the colonial tradition would be attached to the champion of anticolonialism.

More moderate was the attack that

drew strength from the unilateral character of the Monroe Doctrine. This argument even accepted the necessity of giving American protection to Western Europe, but it precluded action in cooperation with any other country. As presented effectively by Professor Curtis Nettels, the United States acted alone in 1823, not in conjunction with Britain, or even any Latin American nation. Why violate this tradition by engaging in an alliance that might limit American freedom of action, and hence the effectiveness of American power? It would be far better for Europeans themselves, as Taft claimed on the Senate floor, if the United States would throw the protective mantle of the Monroe Doctrine around Western Europe but remain free to interpret this enlarged Monroe Doctrine unfettered by any ties. This move would have a greater deterrent effect upon Soviet expansionism than the ratification of the treaty itself. To emphasize this point, Taft in collaboration with Senator Flanders introduced a resolution extending the Monroe Doctrine to Western Europe as a substitute for the North Atlantic Treaty. Although this resolution never went beyond the Committee on Foreign Relations, it reflected the power possessed by the slogans of isolationism.

The counterattack of the Administration spokesmen and their allies in the Senate was prepared well in advance of the actual inquisition. Defense of the treaty as a fulfillment of the Monroe Doctrine had as its first proposition the fact that the Doctrine itself had stretched the original boundaries of isolation. Secretary Acheson pointedly announced that "For more than a century and a quarter this Government has contributed to the peace of the Americas by making clear that it would regard an attack on any

American state as an attack on itself." The elasticity of the disorders of isolationism was thereby established.

Although the Doctrine was promulgated unilaterally, every observer of foreign policy would agree that in the twentieth century defense of the American hemisphere had become a matter of multilateral rather than unilateral concern. In the popular Inter-American Treaty of Reciprocal Assistance, signed at Rio de Janeiro in 1947, the United States subscribed to the reshaping of the Monroe Doctrine so that each country might do its share toward preserving the hemisphere from foreign interference. The process of sharing responsibilities of defense was expected to foster greater harmony among the nations and to increase the collective security without in any way conflicting with American traditions of foreign policy.

If the Rio Pact constituted no break with the past, it followed that the North Atlantic Pact might best be presented to the Senate and to the public as a variation of the Rio Pact, and hence a legitimate extension of the Monroe Doctrine. Substantially the same language was employed in both documents. Both spoke of fulfilling democratic ideals; both pledged loyalty to the United Nations Charter; and both contained clauses providing for response to armed attack. In the words of Secretary Acheson, the treaty "lays down principles on which we have acted in this hemisphere since the statement of President Monroe which developed into a similar treaty within the hemisphere."

But if the treaty resembled the Rio Pact, it also resembled the Brussels Pact, which might be readily taken for the type of European alliance held suspect by Washington, Jefferson, and Monroe. Secretary of Defense Johnson, to his

obvious embarrassment, admitted that he
had expressed just this sentiment in an
address to the Daughters of the American Revolution shortly after the framing
of the Brussels alliance and prior to his
appointment to office. While he later
disavowed this conception, his initial
reaction suggested the hazards awaiting
the North Atlantic Treaty should it become involved with Brussels in the
public mind.

To avoid this conclusion, the treaty's
supporters had to link Western Europe
with America without making it appear
that this link would bind the United
States to a European alliance. This was
accomplished by including the western
part of Europe within the Monroe Doctrine system. For all practical purposes,
they treated the Atlantic Ocean in the
twentieth century as little wider than
American statesman of the nineteenth
century considered the Caribbean Sea.
If American values and zone of security
could be transported and extended to
Latin America in 1823 without violating
the tradition of isolationism, it seemed
reasonable that they could cross the Atlantic in 1949 when the world had
shrunk to a fraction of its earlier size.

The phraseology of the text of the
North Atlantic Treaty served this purpose well. The preamble stated explic-
itly that the parties to the treaty have
a "common heritage and civilization . . .
founded on the principles of democracy,
individual liberty, and the rule of law"
which would be protected and promoted
by the treaty. According to Secretary
Acheson, "There is a community of spirit,
a community of history, and a community of interest in these Atlantic countries." Statements of this sort helped to
create a rubric that could shelter Americans and Europeans alike. The difference between the hemispheres still ex-

isted, but it was no longer the Atlantic
Ocean but an Iron Curtain that separated the United States from the Old
World. The doctrine of the two spheres
remained intact.

If the Administration had difficulty
convincing skeptics that the treaty was
a natural extension of the Monroe Doctrine, it could at least exploit its similarity to the Rio Pact. The task of proving
that the North Atlantic Treaty did not
really provide for a military alliance was
immensely more difficult, especially
when the term "Atlantic Alliance" was
in common use from the beginning. And
yet to accept this description would
mean the subjection of the treaty to the
suspicions raised by the words of Washington, Jefferson, and Monroe. When
Secretary of Defense Johnson, as a private citizen, told the Daughters of the
American Revolution that military alliances were not in the tradition of the
United States, he was only echoing sen-
timents expressed repeatedly at count-
less patriotic gatherings over the years.
The embarrassment he suffered as Secretary of Defense was not due to his
expression of this sentiment, but to his
associating military alliances with the
Brussels Pact, and, by implication, with
the North Atlantic Pact.

There was an alternative, however, to
a flat denial of any relationships between
the treaty and European military alliances. As phrased by prominent private
witnesses, the Administration should
proclaim boldly that the treaty "will be
a departure from a very old and revered
foreign policy of the United States"
made necessary by the exigencies of the
times. In order to turn aside the inevitable charge of "entangling alliance,"
the pact's defenders should then attempt
to endow the pact with the posthumous
blessings of the Founding Fathers. "The

world has gone through such a revolutionary change in the last few years," asserted Will L. Clayton, president of the Atlantic Union Committee, "that I cannot help feeling that if George Washington and our other forefathers lived in the present time, they would do exactly what we are doing." By regarding the exhortations of Washington and Jefferson as applicable to problems of their own generation and by utilizing qualifications in their speeches that would free one generation from the dictates of its predecessor, the Administration might be able to marshal the shades of the Founding Fathers to support the new foreign policy.

Nevertheless, an open welcome to America's participation in a military alliance would present the treaty with too many pitfalls. While the spirit of the Founding Fathers might be accommodated to changed circumstances, their words remained the same. Even if George Washington did soften his judgments on alliances to admit the propriety of "temporary alliances for extraordinary emergencies," how could this pact be lodged under this caveat? The North Atlantic Treaty was to be of twenty years' duration, and hence an obvious case of a permanent attachment. Unquestionably, the opponents of the treaty would have used this arguing point with greater success than they actually enjoyed if the Administration had been willing to define the treaty as a military alliance.

The vulnerability of the idea of a military alliance was not limited to its time span. The treaty's enemies could also make a clear causal connection with the military assistance program which the Administration was then devising for the member nations, and thereby exhibit to the public a new set of images, each

with unpleasant connotations. Military assistance linked with an alliance suggests a perpetual financial drain upon the American taxpayer. Under this construction Article 3 of the treaty, calling for "continuous and effective self-help and mutual aid," could be cited as a vehicle for unlimited shipments of arms and armaments by the United States to its allies. Indeed, these charges were leveled, though rendered harmless by the reply that the treaty implied no commitment to a military assistance program.

The real fear of the treaty's supporters in the Administration and in the Senate was not of the potentially high cost of such aid but of the cumulative effect upon the public mind of military aid plus military alliance. To sympathetic as well as hostile witnesses this would add up to war. A typical reaction was that of Mrs. Clifford A. Bender, a Methodist Church spokesman: "History indicates that the most that can be achieved by military alliances is a temporary balance of power, while they eventually give rise to increasing insecurity and a menacing arms race, ending in war."

Once the association of treaty, alliance, and war had been established, new complications arose, involving infringements upon Constitutional powers. One of the criticisms of the treaty that Senators Donnell and Watkins made before the press, the Committee on Foreign Relations, and the Congress, concerned the potential usurpation of Congressional responsibility for declaring war. According to this line of argument, Article 5 would force the United States into war, inasmuch as an attack on one was to be considered an attack on all. The Congress, in a crisis, would have no choice except to take military action under the terms of the entangling alliance that would place the war-making power either at the discretion of any one or more of eleven allies or at the discretion of the President, who as Commander-in-Chief could use armed forces in the event of a bombing of Paris much as he would use it after a bombing of New York or Pearl Harbor. They further pointed out that the highly regarded Rio Pact at least noted in Article 20 that "no state shall be required to use armed force without its consent."

These questions required considerable skill in parrying. The concept of an alliance was truly a Pandora's box containing the plagues of war, sabotage of the Constitution, raid on the United States Treasury, etc. For all the caution displayed by the managers of the pact, some of those plagues were bound to escape even if the box officially remained closed.

The Administration made every effort in the hearings, nevertheless, to introduce the treaty as a plan completely opposed to the spirit and structure of the usual military alliance. Since the charge itself could not be concealed — indeed it had been bruited about by the press for weeks prior to the hearings — the Chairman of the Committee on Foreign Relations would present the accusation to each friendly witness and then help him demolish it. "It is our contention," asserted Senator Connally, "that this is in no way a military alliance in the sense of a military alliance of the past hundred years. This treaty is purely one of defense. It does not contemplate conquest; it does not contemplate aggression."

To supplement this claim with something more than the enthusiasm of the Chairman or the luster of the famous names that testified for the pact, the Administration placed great emphasis on the fact that European alliances were inherently aggressive. The Holy Alliance of 1815, for example, provided that the parties "will on all occasions and in all places, lend each other aid and assistance."

None of this obloquy could be attached to the treaty at hand because it was the instrument of democratic nations that would never sanction any "secret deals" of the type associated with the typical bilateral alliances and ententes. The text of the North Atlantic Treaty carries no suggestion of "alliance or aggression." It meant exactly what it said. It was directed solely against aggression, against any attempt to change the *status quo* by force, but it was not directed against any nation. Furthermore, there was no automatic declaration of war involved, even if a blatant attack were made upon a signatory power directly endangering America's security. The wording of Article 5 was carefully chosen so that to Europeans it might sound as if America was promising the same protection offered in the Brussels Pact, while to Americans it would promise faithful observance of the constitutional processes involved in declaring war. Note the distinction between the two pacts in this regard: in the event of attack the members of the Brussels treaty will "afford the Party so attacked all the military and other aid and assistance *in their power*," while the North Atlantic Treaty qualified this to the extent that every member will take "*such action as it deems necessary*, including the use of armed force, to restore and maintain the security of the North Atlantic area."

The language of Article 5 was not a major asset to the pact's cause even under the most charitable interpretation, and its defenders realized this fully. Their objective, therefore, was to draw attention away from the military functions of the treaty, and once again they succeeded in turning the language of isolationists to their own advantage. The twenty-year life of the pact which would have been so objectionable in an alliance was celebrated as proof that the cooperation envisaged in the treaty was not essentially military in nature. According to Mr. John Foster Dulles, most military alliances are matters of "temporary expediency" in pursuit of individual and often antagonistic ambitions. The pact, on the other hand, grew naturally out of a recognition on the part of its constituent members of a common unity and purpose. In other words, the emphasis in the text of the treaty was placed as much on the promotion of stability, the assurance of well-being, the safeguarding of their common heritage, and the encouragement of economic collaboration as on the guarantees against external aggression.

Of the many participants in the debates over the nature of the treaty, there were few who did not commit themselves unreservedly, either defending it against every attack or attacking every defense without regard for the merits of specific arguments. An exception seemed to be Senator Hickenlooper, who announced himself in favor of the treaty but not in favor of the many circumlocutions he had listened to. Inasmuch as the objectives of the treaty were military, getting "ourselves and our allies in a sufficient position so we can and will fight under those eventual last-ditch conditions," he believed that it would be unwise not to recognize the treaty for what it was — a military alliance. As far as he was concerned a reversal in American foreign policy was necessary, and asserting that this pact was in no way a military alliance would only make it more difficult for both the

American public and the allies to understand America's new responsibilities.

Despite their willingness to play with words, the friends of the pact did not appear to be playing a cynical game with the Senate or with the public. The distinctions between the North Atlantic Treaty and a military alliance had more than a semantic meaning for them, even though many had trouble articulating those distinctions. In effect, the connotations of the term, "military alliance," did violence to their conception of the purpose of the pact, and any such association would be a misstatement of fact as well as an obstacle in the way of public acceptance. To Senator Henry Cabot Lodge, Jr., for example, a military alliance meant quite plainly "an aggressive combination of nations who are going out on the rampage to attack and oppress people . . . in a spirit of cynicism and opportunism, without regard to any common idealistic values." To observers of this mind, terms such as "partnership for peace" or "broad partnership for security" represent not merely euphemisms designed to lull the public but ideals directly in the American tradition of foreign relations.

The North Atlantic Treaty was ultimately accepted on terms laid down by the Government. On July 21, 1949, the Senate approved the treaty 82 to 13, a majority large enough to be hailed as an impressive vote of confidence in a milestone of America's foreign policy. It signified that the Senate Committee on Foreign Relations' report on the treaty convinced isolationists that the past conformed with the spirit of the Monroe Doctrine and had nothing in common with the old European military alliances. In brief, the Government succeeded in invoking the shibboleths of isolationism to win acceptance of a policy that marked a departure from the isolationist traditions.

While the spokesmen for the treaty obviously recognized the speciousness of some of the claims, it was equally obvious that their arguments were based on something more than political expediency. They interpreted the isolationist symbols to justify a new turn in foreign policy but not a new policy. Though they spoke for foreign entanglements and accepted the balance-of-power philosophy, they did so in the name of the Founding Fathers and of their concern for American security.

The symbols that they exploited might have destroyed the concept of the North Atlantic Treaty, and possibly America's leadership in world affairs. Instead, the language of an old policy served to open new vistas for the free world. There were dangers in this method. The symbols of isolationism could be used differently at another time, and the frequency of the "Great Debates" in the succeeding years attests to the latent power of isolationism. Furthermore, the future of NATO was to be complicated because of the circumlocutions and ambiguities of the treaty. But whatever the language employed in 1949, Europeans at last knew that the vast weight America could wield in international politics had swung behind them.

Armin Rappaport: THE AMERICAN REVOLUTION OF 1949

Armin Rappaport, Professor of History at the University of California at Berkeley, acclaimed the signing of the Treaty as a revolution in American foreign policy, all the more extraordinary in view of the insistent isolationism of the twentieth century. With this treaty the nation had broken the hold of isolationism on its foreign policy and joined an organization which is "the rock on which rests the safety and the security of the Atlantic Community."

ON 4 April 1949, in Washington, D. C., American foreign policy underwent a revolution. On that day, Dean Acheson, the Secretary of State, with the American President and Vice-President looking on, affixed his signature at the end of the fourteen articles of the North Atlantic Treaty, thereby joining with Canada and the ten original European NATO countries in a defensive alliance. Some three months later, on 21 July, the United States Senate, by an overwhelming vote of 82 to 13, provided legislative approval.

The revolution lay in the fact that the United States pledged its resources to defend the territory of the co-signatories — whether that territory was contiguous to the United States as in the case of Canada or thousands of miles away. The commitment was clearly embodied in Article 5 of the Treaty: "The Parties agree that an armed attack against one or more of them in Europe or North America shall be considered an attack against them all; and consequently they agree that, if such an armed attack occurs, each of them . . . will assist the

From Armin Rappaport, "The American Revolution of 1949," *NATO Letter* (February, 1964), pp. 3–8. Reprinted with permission of NATO Information Service.

Party or Parties so attacked by taking forthwith, individually and in concert with the other parties, such action as it deems necessary, including the use of armed force . . ."

What, in fact, had happened was that America had departed from a one hundred and fifty-year-old tradition and stood ready to abandon the precepts of the Founding Fathers. Both George Washington in his "Farewell Address" and Thomas Jefferson in his Inaugural Address had laid the foundations of a foreign policy of non-entanglement which developed into articles of faith from which few Americans strayed. Said George Washington on 17 September 1796, in his valedictory to the American people:

Why, by inter-weaving our destiny with that of any part of Europe, entangle our peace and property in the toils of European ambition, rivalship, interest, humour, or caprice? It is our true policy to steer clear of permanent alliances with any portion of the foreign world.

And Thomas Jefferson, upon assuming office on 4 March 1801, stated what he considered

the essential principles of our government, and consequently those which ought to shape its Administration . . . ; peace, commerce and honest friendship with all nations, entangling alliances with none. . . .

John Adams, James Madison, James Monroe, and other statesmen of the young republic agreed with these principles. Few people regretted the termination of the Franco-American alliance by Congress in 1798 and by treaty with France in 1880. No one questioned the value of France's aid during the war with Great Britain; indeed, it was widely

acknowledged that without French assistance victory would have been impossible. The alliance, however, had threatened to drag the young American republic into European conflicts in the 1790's, and its abrogation was heartily welcomed. It was the first alliance in American history and was to be the last until the North Atlantic Treaty was signed one hundred and fifty-one years later.

Throughout the nineteenth century, the United States steered clear of involvement in foreign adventures. Henry Clay turned aside the appeal for assistance by the Hungarian patriot, Louis Kossuth, with the remark that it would be best for the United States to stay out of the "distant wars of Europe." Senator James Mason of Virginia urged "avoiding all alliances, whether transient or permanent," and President Zachary Taylor recalled "the voice of our own beloved Washington to abstain from entangling alliances." Whigs and Democrats joined in asserting their faith in this basic precept of American policy. Separation from Europe was not a party issue.

There is no clearer evidence of America's resolve to shy away from European involvement than the pronouncement of the Monroe Doctrine in December 1823 and subsequently the complete acceptance of the ideas of the Doctrine by all parties, factions, and sections in the United States. President Monroe, in his annual message to Congress, says, "In the wars of the European powers in matters relating to themselves, we have never taken any part, nor does it comport with our policy so to do . . . Our policy in regard to Europe, . . . is, not to interfere in the national concerns of any of its powers." Here, stated in classic form, was the doctrine of the two spheres and the separation of the two worlds, old and new, American and European, and of the determination of the American people to maintain the distance between the two. Monroe was expressing only what most Americans believed, and his words were echoed thereafter frequently and regularly.

So strongly ingrained was the Washingtonian dictum regarding alliances that even when the United States found it desirable to go to war in 1917 alongside France and Britain, President Wilson insisted that no alliance be made with the co-belligerents. The United States remained an "associated," not an allied power. Senator William E. Borah was only following the tradition and reflecting a general view when he said, "I seek or accept no alliances. I obligate this Government to no other power."

Seen in the light of these precedents, the American action in 1949 appears truly revolutionary. The revolutionary quality can best be appreciated by a consideration of the history of the twenty years preceding America's entry into the Second World War. During those years, the American people and government clung more devoutly than ever before in their history to the "no entanglement no involvement" precept. They were not isolationist. Quite the reverse. Americans travelled abroad in those two decades in great numbers. American representatives participated in many international congresses and conferences and signed numerous treaties and agreements: the naval treaties of 1922, 1927 and 1930; the Kellogg-Briand Pact; and many others. American businessmen engaged in trade with every part of the globe, and American bankers extended loans to almost every civilized nation of the world. But what Americans, government and people, refused to do was to promise military aid and assistance in the event of an attack

by an aggressor nation. What the United States said to Europe was that an attack upon one shall *not* be considered an attack upon the United States; indeed, that such an attack did not concern them.

President Wilson's hope that the United States would join the League of Nations after the First World War and thereby help to guarantee the peace of the world was dashed by the United States Senate which refused to sanction a commitment to halt a future aggressor. The Senate was reflecting the sentiment of a large portion of the American people as expressed by a Boston newspaper in 1919 which noted that the League "Surrenders the Monroe Doctrine; Flaunts Washington's Warning; Entangles us in European and Asiatic Intrigues; Sends Our Boys to Fight Throughout the World . . ." In his first message to Congress in 1921, President Harding drew applause with the words, "In the existing League of Nations with its super powers, the republic will have no part."

To be sure, America did not continue its alienation from the League and soon began attending various League-sponsored Conferences — those dealing, for example, with opium traffic, customs formalities, anthrax, passport control, obscene publications, and the like — but they were all of a non-political nature. In October 1931, on the occasion of the League Council's deliberations on the Sino-Japanese dispute over Manchuria, an American representative did sit with the League Council. He was, however, carefully instructed to act only as "observer and auditor" and to refrain from voting on any issues and from making any commitments for the United States. But even this limited participation aroused misgivings and fears in America. Soon the warnings from all parts of the United States of the dangers of transgressing the injunctions of the Founding Fathers and tradition of a century of history caused Secretary of State Henry L. Stimson to remove his delegate from the Council table. Never again did an American join a League discussion on political affairs.

Every treaty or agreement signed by the United States during the two decades studiously and deliberately avoided any reference to the use of force against a treaty violator. Consultations and moral disapprobation, as in the Pact of Paris for the outlawry of war, were the only sanctions foreseen. Moreover, every conference for the limitation of armaments attended by the United States in the same period just as carefully omitted any mention of a guarantee of security to nations which reduced armaments. To every plea by the European continental nations that disarmament must be preceded by a guarantee of security, the United States turned a deaf ear. To the Belgian Prime Minister's suggestion, "Give us an assurance of safety and we Belgians will gladly dismiss our soldiers," President Herbert Hoover, some years later, offered America's answer,

The European nations have by the Covenant of the League of Nations agreed that if nations fail to settle their differences peaceably then force should be applied by other nations to compel them to be reasonable. We have refused to travel this road.

The reasons for the American position are not obscure. Americans came out of the First World War deeply disillusioned. They had intervened in 1917 to help defeat militarism, colonialism, and imperialism as personified in the Kaiser's Germany. They had fought to ensure a victory for democracy, liberty and Western civilization as embodied in the Allied cause. When they learned after the war

that the Allies had made secret treaties during the war for dividing the spoils of victory and when they read of the squabbling at the Paris Peace Conference over the carcass of the German empire, they wondered if the fight had not been in vain.

The revelations from Czarist archives published by the Bolshevik government after the revolution further revolted the American people. The record revealed conversations and negotiations in the years before the war between France and Russia which indicated that those nations bore some of the responsibility for the coming of the war. Revelations from German archives also threw some of the blame for the war on the Allied powers. Quite naturally Americans said, never again will we involve ourselves in Europe's imbroglios or commit our resources to its defence.

It is against this backdrop that the American reaction to the coming of the Second World War must be assessed. As Americans observed the events in Europe and in Asia in the 1930s, a deep uneasiness possessed them. They were shocked to read of Japan's invasion of China, Mussolini's attack upon Ethiopia, and Hitler's mad conduct in Germany and in the neighbouring countries. The world seemed to be collapsing and all the things America held dear — justice, decency, honesty, law — were being threatened with extinction. Yet, deeper than the feeling of uneasiness was the resolution that the United States must not be dragged into another conflict. As the thirties moved on, the collective mind of America was geared to recalling the futility of 1917–18 and of the crusade to save the world for democracy. Books such as Walter Millis's *Road to War*, Edwin Borchard's *Neutrality for the United States*, and C. Hartley Grattan's

Why We Fought; articles such as *Fortune's* "Arms and the Men"; speeches and statements by writers and politicians — all warned Americans, "Do not let it happen again." The liberal New York weekly magazine, *Nation,* summed up the public attitude in an issue of 16 October 1935:

As a people we have little sympathy for the inhumanity of Italian Fascism. We are shocked and indignant at Mussolini's brazen invasion of Ethiopia. But the experience of one war fought for what we believed to be the highest of idealistic principles has convinced us, rightly or wrongly, that the harm resulting from Il Duce's mad adventure will be slight compared with the havoc that would be wrought by another world conflict. Whatever may happen we are determined that American youth shall not again be sacrificed. . . .

The extent of America's determination not to become involved again in a European war may be seen in the series of neutrality acts passed by the United States Congress between 1935 and 1937. These statutes, three in number, were designed to prevent the United States from getting involved in any war which might break out as a result of the anarchic conditions in Europe and Asia. Believing that involvement in the First World War stemmed from the extensive contacts by American citizens with the belligerents, the laws circumscribed the actions of Americans in a future war. They would not be permitted to export arms, ammunition, or implements of war; to lend money or extend credit to the belligerents; to travel on belligerent passenger ships; and to sail American vessels into war zones. All these prohibitions were calculated to prevent Americans from establishing an economic or emotional stake in the cause of either belligerent which might lead, as we believed

to have been the case in 1917, to their participation.

Americans applauded the wisdom of their congressional representatives and, as one prominent American journal described the speed with which the first of these acts went through Congress, "It dramatizes the American peoples' passionate abhorrence of war." Yet twelve years after the enactment of these statutes, the American Secretary of State, reflecting the wishes of the vast majority of the American people who had a few years earlier so abhorred war, put his signature on the document pledging the nation to fight. Here, indeed, was a momentous revolution.

The reason is plain to see. The American people had fought a long, gruelling and costly war and out of the death, destruction and devastation had come the realization that the price of fighting and winning a war was greater than the risk of preventing it by a frank and direct warning to a would-be aggressor. As President Harry S. Truman noted on the occasion of the signing of the Treaty: "If [this document] had existed in 1914 and 1939, supported by the nations who are represented today, I believe it would have prevented the acts of aggression which led to two world wars." Americans became aware, too, that their security lay in Europe, that their frontier was on the Rhine, and that the Atlantic Ocean was not the barrier it was once thought to be but a highway which inexorably bound America to Europe.

A State Department spokesman put the matter succinctly:

The security of the United States would again be seriously endangered if the entire European continent were once more to come under the domination of a power or an association of powers antagonistic to the United States. Continental Europe was lost to the

Allied Powers in the Second World War before the United States became an active par-
ticipant. It was regained at great risk and
at an enormous loss of lives and expenditure
of material and money. Today, the weakened condition in which the nations of
Europe find themselves as a result of the destruction and privation of war has afforded
a golden opportunity for a new aggressor. It
is clear in this case — as it is clear, in retro-
spect, in the case of Nazi Germany — that
dominance of the European continent, once
attained and consolidated, could be the first
step in a large plan of attack on Great
Britain, and then on the United States and
the rest of the Western Hemisphere. The
problems created by this possibility of progressive and sustained aggression are legiti-
mately the concern of United States security
planning. The maintenance of the freedom
and independence of the countries of Western Europe is of pre-eminent importance.
It is believed essential to the security of the
United States, therefore, that it consolidate
the friendship and support which it now en-
joys from free and friendly nations, . . . the
last two great wars have proved that a major
conflict in Europe would inevitably involve
the United States. The North Atlantic Pact
. . . is designed to give assurance that in the
case of such a war there will be a coordinated
defence . . .

Americans, also, came to accept the
fact that they were part of an Atlantic
community sharing common ideals and
aspirations and cherishing liberty and
democracy, that they had an obligation
to contribute to the community's defence
and survival against the new authorita-
rian aggressor in the east. It had, in fact,
taken two wars in one generation to
teach Americans the lessons which led
them to accept their true international
responsibilities. One war had disillusioned them; the second has chastened
them.

As was to be expected, the European
Allies rejoiced. The United States had,
at last, joined in the defence of Western
civilization and expressions of gratitude
descended upon Washington from many
European capitals. Yet as was also to be
expected, some statesmen and publicists
were sceptical. They wondered whether
America would, in fact, provide the vast
military resources to implement the
treaty. It quickly became clear that the
American commitment would be carried
out. On 6 October 1949, the Congress
authorized the expenditure of $1,341,-
010,000 for military assistance for the
period ending 30 June 1950 — one billion
of it earmarked for the North Atlantic
Treaty Organization. On 9 September
1950, President Truman announced the
dispatch of four United States army divisions to Europe to be placed at NATO's
disposal, and in December, General
Dwight D. Eisenhower was designated
Supreme Commander, Allied Powers,
Europe.

To this commitment the American
people and government have held. Major
elements of the United States army, air
force and navy are deployed in Western
Europe and funds have been annually
provided to implement Article 3: "In
order more effectively to achieve the objectives of the Treaty, the Parties, separately and jointly, by means of continuous and effective self-help and mutual
aid, will maintain and develop their individual and collective capacity to resist
armed attack."

Even during the dark winter of 1950–
51 when U. S. troops suffered heavy
reverses in Korea and many Americans,
deeply disappointed and frustrated,
called for a curtailment of America's
far-flung responsibilities, there was no
change in policy. The sombre voice of
former President Hoover in December
1950, warning the American people that
Europe could not be defended in the
face of the Soviet Union's preponderant
land power and urging the creation of a

"Gibraltar of the West" in America, did not cause an alteration in the stern resolve to maintain the integrity of NATO. Nor did a similar plea by the respected Senator Robert A. Taft.

NATO is the rock on which rests the safety and security of the Atlantic community. While every avenue must be explored for easing the tension and diminishing the hostility between East and West, NATO's guard must not once be let down; it is our sword and shield. With it, the peace has been maintained. America's share in maintaining the peace,

a crucial share, has been made possible because, as President Truman has said,

We were ready to break with tradition and enter into a peacetime military alliance; because we had been ready to assume not only our share but the leadership in the forging of joint forces; because we had recognized that the peace of the world would best be served by a Europe that was strong and united, and that therefore European unity and European strength were the best guarantees for the prevention of another major war.

David Horowitz: THE DIVISION OF EUROPE

In his extended critique of American foreign policy in the Cold War entitled The Free World Colossus, *David Horowitz, a former Woodrow Wilson Fellow of the University of California at Berkeley, argues that the policy of containment was little more than a refusal to permit the Soviet Union to maintain the sphere of influence in Europe that the war had won for her. The United States, and not the Soviet Union, originated the Cold War by an expansionist policy based on "America's atomic monopoly and preponderance of economic power."*

THE key elements of U.S. power, as seen by Forrestal and Baruch and obvious to anyone, were atomic monopoly and preponderance of economic power; control of all the seas, the world's largest fleet, and a worldwide network of hundreds of bases made these powers globally operative. It is not to be overlooked, moreover, that a lack of these elements constituted the basis of Soviet weakness; indeed, Baruch's proposal depended on the dual assumptions that the U.S. had the capacity to carry out such a program *and* that preclusive buying of raw materials would have a significant effect on the Soviet economy.

It is not surprising, therefore, to find that Lippmann began his assault on the policy of containment, not with a critique of legalistic attitudes, but by examining the assumption that the Soviet Union was weak, even collapsing, and did not *have* to be dealt with as a major power. Lippmann initiated his whole analysis with these words:

We must begin with the disturbing fact that Mr. X's conclusions depend upon the optimistic prediction that the "Soviet power . . . bears within itself the seeds of its own decay, and that the sprouting of these seeds is well advanced," that if "anything were ever to occur to disrupt the unity and the efficacy

From *The Free World Colossus* by David Horowitz, pp. 248–252, 255–262. Copyright © David Horowitz, 1965. Reprinted by permission of Hill and Wang, Inc. and of MacGibbon & Kee Ltd.

of the Party as a political instrument, Soviet Russia might be changed overnight [*sic*] from one of the strongest to one of the weakest and most pitiable of national societies;" and "that Soviet society may well [*sic*] contain deficiencies which will eventually weaken its own total potential."

Of this optimistic prediction Mr. X himself says that "it cannot be proved. And it cannot be disproved." Nevertheless, he concludes that the United States should construct its policy on the assumption that the Soviet power is inherently weak and impermanent, and that this unproved assumption warrants our entering "with reasonable confidence upon a policy of firm containment . . ."

Having pinpointed Kennan's estimate of the weakness and impermanence of Soviet power as the orienting basis of Kennan's strategy, Lippmann declared:

I do not find much ground for reasonable confidence in a policy which can be successful only if the most optimistic prediction should prove to be true. Surely a sound policy must be addressed to the worst and hardest that may be judged to be probable, and not to the best and easiest that may be possible.

Here is the heart of the dispute.

Now the significance of the "X" article in the shaping of United States foreign policy must not be overlooked. Kennan was the Director of the newly formed Policy Planning Staff of the State Department.

Thus, as Lippmann noted in the introduction to his analysis, once Mr. X was identified as George Kennan,

Mr. X's article was no longer just one more report on the Soviet régime and what to do about it. It was an event, announcing that the Department of State had made up its mind, and was prepared to disclose to the American people, to the world at large, and of course also to the Kremlin, the estimates, the calculations and the conclusions on which the Department was basing its plans.

It takes little imagination to speculate on the considerations and possibilities that might have been entertained by United States (and British) leaders at the time. Given a working estimate that the Soviet régime was on the brink of collapse, the necessity for achieving a compromise settlement would recede into the background. With the atomic monopoly of the West intact, and expected to remain so for five to ten years, certain risks could be taken. The situation presented Western leaders with the opportunity, among others, to be rid of a hated and feared régime, ideology and social system, ruled by a group of men who were at best difficult to live with, and at worst constituted a formidable threat to Western interests, in many eyes, to Western survival.

Against the advantages of the "hard line" of containment, moreover, there were certain disadvantages, from the standpoint of the American leadership, in seeking a negotiated settlement which would end the occupation of Eastern Europe. In the first place, any settlement to have been acceptable to the Soviets, would have had to offer them substantial benefits, as Lippmann pointed out, to compensate for what would have been "a deep reduction of [their] present power and influence in Europe."

But any compensation for Soviet loss of power in Europe must have entailed the strengthening of Soviet power at home. And this was something that American leaders had been reluctant to do, even before the Second World War had ended. On January 3, 1945, the Soviet Government had filed its first formal request for a post-war credit. Molotov's memorandum asked for long-term credits to the amount of $6 billion, to be paid back over thirty years at two and one-quarter per cent.

The memorandum was given to Ambassador Harriman, who advised Washington at the time, that the U.S. ought to do everything it could to assist the Soviet Union to develop a sound economy by credits. For he explained that he was convinced ". . . that the sooner the Soviet Union can develop a decent life for its people the more tolerant they will become." Unfortunately this far seeing advice was neither heeded in Washington, nor maintained by Harriman. Three months later, in April, Harriman described the "enormous plans" for Russian industrial expansion, and mentioned their request for a $6 billion credit to start on these vast projects, but he dropped the question as to whether "our basic interest might better be served by increasing our trade with other parts of the world rather than giving preference to the Soviet Union as a source of supply . . . our experience has incontrovertibly proved that it is not possible to bank general good will in Moscow and I agree with the Department [of State] that we should retain current control of these credits in order to be in a position to protect American vital interests in the formulative period immediately following the war."

Initial reluctance to bolster the Soviet system was undoubtedy re-enforced by the policy (and predictions) of containment, which looked towards a strangling of Soviet power from without rather than a fostering of healthy forces from within. Moreover, concentrating on Western build-up, it must have been felt, would bolster forces whose friendship was certain, while at the same time exerting strong pressures on the Soviet Union to divert must of its energies to a counter build-up, particularly in East Europe, where it was busy taking by force what it could not borrow from the West. Thus the policy of containment promised to be doubly advantageous, strengthening the West, while encouraging Soviet power, which was already dangerously strained, to over-extend and perhaps over-strain itself, thereby precipitating its final collapse.

Such expectations proved false, however, and Soviet power strengthened itself (at a severe human cost) while tightening its grip on East Europe. Against the fact that a reconstructed Western Europe did not become Communist, therefore, would have to be weighed (if one were to make such a judgement) the fact that Eastern Europe did, an eventuality that might not have occurred if a settlement, meaning withdrawal, had been reached.

In gauging to what extent *in fact* Western leaders did not follow Lippmann's approach to settlement because they expected and indeed wished to promote Soviet collapse, it is useful to focus on a few concrete and crucial policy statements and proposals, which engage the substantive issues of the early cold war. In particular, it will be necessary to determine whether Western appeals to the Soviet Union for cooperation towards the making of a settlement were merely specious, or whether they contained genuine overtures to the Soviet rulers to recognize their own self-interest in an Atomic Age, in international stability and peace.

*   *   *

It is by no means insignificant, that the only cabinet member to actively oppose the Truman-Byrnes diplomatic offensive, Henry Wallace, held precisely the same estimate for precisely the same reasons, which he set forth in his famous letter to Truman in 1946.

To Administration leaders, beguiled by the newly evolved policy of creating "situations of strength," however, even the explosion of the Soviet A-bomb did not compel a shift from optimism to realism. In a major address in Berkeley, California in March 1950, Acheson countered appeals from many quarters to resume high level discussions with the Soviet Union, in light of the changed situation.

It was evident from Acheson's remarks, that the Administration did not hold the general view that the power situation had, in fact, significantly changed. The Russians could not have had a large nuclear stockpile, nor extensive means to deliver nuclear bombs to the continental U.S. Moreover, the U.S. had already begun plans for an H-bomb, which would be a thousand times more powerful than the A-bomb. In any case, Acheson's view of coexistence with the Soviets as expressed in his speech did not indicate that he suspected that a situation was rapidly developing in which such a course would be a compelling necessity.

Like Churchill before him, Acheson set forth the steps which the Soviet Union would have to take unilaterally to "permit [sic] the rational and peaceful development of the coexistence of their system and ours." The steps included change of their position on the U.N. and outstanding peace treaties, withdrawal from East Europe, agreement to "realistic and effective" arrangements for control of atomic weapons, stopping the efforts of the national communist parties to overthrow régimes in any country which is outwardly friendly to the Soviet Union and stopping the distortion of motives of others through false propaganda that speaks of a "capitalist encirclement" and of the U.S. craftily and systematically plotting another world war. As James Reston observed, if the Soviets accepted these conditions "they would virtually cease to be Communists." Once again the Soviet Union was being asked to surrender its position as a condition for entering serious negotiations. It was being asked to "cooperate" not in making a compromise settlement, but in securing the achievement of Western objectives.

Acheson's continued confidence, his disinterest in attempts to settle the conflict with Russia, his apparent lack of concern for the growing consolidation of the division of Europe, cannot be explained merely by the extent to which American officials discounted the immediate significance of the Soviet nuclear test, however. For to put the Soviet achievement of nuclear capability five to ten years in the future as they did, would be to offer a strong argument in favor of negotiations in the present, while the United States still had its immense nuclear advantage as a bargaining factor. Such an argument would be undermined, on the other hand, if the Soviet power position was expected to decline, as indeed the containment thesis had predicted. The failure of American leaders to attempt to capitalize their immense power advantage in the early cold war years through negotiation, can only mean that they expected to achieve their purposes without negotiation. (The same conclusion is reached by a sympathetic critic of the Achesonian doctrine of "negotiation from strength," who has written: "The hope held out in Acheson's words is of agreements registering acceptance of a situation that has been changed by other means. . . .")

This is also the conclusion reached by the historian William Appleman Williams, proceeding from slightly different considerations:

The emphasis [of American leaders] on open-door expansion [in regard to the Marshall Plan and the Truman Doctrine] and the assumption of the inevitable downfall of the Soviet Union suggest that American leaders were not motivated solely by fear of

Russian expansion. Their plan for dealing with the possibility that the Soviet Union would accept the Marshall Plan indicated this. Kennan thought the possibility could be handled, even if it materialized, by requiring Russia to divert resources from its own recovery to the aid of Western Europe . . . viewed in the light of his assumption [in the "X" article] that American power would force Russia to give way, Kennan's advice on how to "play it straight" suggests that American leaders thought it was basically a matter of time until the Russian problem was solved. Their continued remarks discounting the probability of Russian attack point in the same direction.

In introducing the specter of Soviet expansion as a possible motivation for American policy, Williams touches on what is probably the main point of resistance to the above line of argument. In fact, however, the whole orthodox conception of American policy towards the Soviet Union as a policy of response, is undermined by a careful consideration of the pivotal events of this period between the explosion of the Soviet A-bomb and the war in Korea.

At this moment in cold war history, the American defense budget was at the low post-war level of $13 billion (still, however, more than 30 per cent of the $39.5 billion budget). The Russians had ended their blockade of Berlin the preceding May and thus eased their pressure against the weakest point along the NATO front in Europe. The NATO pact itself had been signed and ratified and the first American arms aid sent to the member countries.

Not only was the Western position in Europe stronger than it had been during the previous four years, but a consensus of responsible observers had seen in the approaching end to American atomic monopoly an opportunity to open serious negotiations to halt the arms race and

pacify the cold war conflict. In addition to Lippmann, Senators Tydings and Mac-Mahon (chairman of the Joint Committee on Atomic Energy) called for imaginative diplomatic action, while the New York *Herald Tribune* editorialized (in February) that there was a feeling among "millions of Americans that there must be a new approach to the Soviet Union in order to close the horrible vistas" ahead. At the same time, Harrison Salisbury was allowed to report from Russia that some Moscow diplomatic quarters believed that the Soviet Government was prepared to meet the U.S. in "a two-power effort to solve the major problems confronting both countries, including the question of atomic controls."

It was in this context that Acheson firmly and publicly shut the door to negotiations towards a constructive settlement, while in Washington a secret decision was taken to embark on a massive rearmament program. Before considering this latter development, however, let us dwell a little more on the historical turn which events took in the spring of 1950, and on the orthodox interpretation of them.

The failure "to grasp the opportunities for a constructive peace settlement" in the spring of 1950, had dire consequences for the future course of the cold war. Indeed, the really intractable problems attending a European settlement may be said to date from this period. For by the time a substantial, if half-hearted attempt to negotiate issues had been made at Geneva in 1955, the Korean War had intervened, the American defense budget had quadrupled in size, and German rearmament within the structure of NATO was well under way.

This disastrous chain of events is easily assimilated into orthodox Western accounts of the cold war, in a way which preserves the "defensive" character and responsive nature of American policy. According to this version of history, the North Korean invasion of South Korea was the first stage in a new program of Soviet expansion, inspired by the Kremlin's recent acquisition of the Atomic Bomb. In the circumstances, the 325 per cent increase in the American defense budget in the next two fiscal years (so that it surpassed the *total* budget prior to the increase) is comprehensible. The same argument would explain the urgency with which U.S. leaders sought to have Western Germany rearmed within the NATO alliance, rather than neutralized and armed defensively on the pattern of Austria. The trouble with this orthodox view, quite apart from the fact that Acheson had already begun his campaign for West German rearmament in 1949, and that Soviet responsibility for the North Korean invasion is still by no means clearly established, is that the American decisions to maintain their opposition to a negotiated settlement and to quadruple the peacetime military budget were taken *at least two months prior to the invasion of South Korea.*

These crucial policy decisions were made in accord with the broad strategy prescribed by a National Security Council Paper (N S C-68), initialled by President Truman in April 1950, which dealt with international relations, particularly with respect to the Soviet Union. The paper, described by Acheson as "one of the great documents in our history" held that there was a basic and probably permanent incompatibility between Communist and democratic philosophies, ". . . that will keep the Communist and non-Communist worlds in conflict into an unforeseeable future [the words are those of the New York *Times* account]." In this

situation, the document held, the U.S. could pursue one of four alternatives (none of which, of course, entailed entering negotiations).

It could do nothing beyond what it already was doing, it could abandon its international commitments and retreat behind "fortress America," it could attempt to forestall danger with a preventive war, or it could undertake a massive rebuilding of its own and the free world's defensive capabilities and adopt an unflinching "will to fight" posture toward its enemies.

This latter course was chosen in the N.S.C. document, which said, in elaboration, that "The nation should think of arms cost in an order of magnitude of $50 billion annually [as opposed to the present $13 billion]."

Thus, in a period of relative international tranquility, amidst admonitions from many distinguished sources to open negotiations towards a settlement of the European and nuclear problems, the U.S. leadership not only reaffirmed the strategic decisions of 1945–7 against negotiations and the use of diplomacy, but opted also for military rearmament on a scale never before witnessed in peacetime.

The secret character of the N.S.C. document puts a severe limit on the conclusions which can be safely drawn from reports of its contents. One seemingly inescapable conclusion, however, is the emptiness of the orthodox view which sees American policy in this period as consisting of responses to Soviet strategies. For while the Korean conflict may have played a role in making possible the actual American military buildup, the *policy decision* to increase the military posture fourfold — with all the consequences that that entailed for the problem of divided Europe — was strategic and not defensive in character.

As long as the N.S.C. document remains secret, the full range of motives behind this plan to quadruple a military posture which had already "contained" Soviet power in Greece, Turkey, Iran and Berlin — insofar as it needed containing — must remain obscure. But if we focus our attention on the NATO build-up in Western Europe, a major element in the strategy of American policy at this time, becomes clear.

NATO had been formed in 1949 not so much to provide a force capable of containing a Soviet land aggression, as to provide a "trip-wire" which would involve the United States and engage U.S. nuclear power. Thus NATO was intended to have only 22 divisions against some 180 estimated Soviet divisions, and could not have prevented the Red Army from marching swiftly to the sea. Then, in February 1952, four years after the Czech *coup* and six months after truce talks had begun in Korea, the NATO allies met in Lisbon and approved a plan which would provide 50 divisions by the end of 1952, 70 by the end of 1953 and 97 by the end of 1954. These quotas were never filled, because the European powers were unimpressed by the immediacy of any threat and were content to rely on the U.S. deterrent if any should arise. One must assume these countries had adequate military intelligence forces, and thus that there was in fact no immediate threat to their security. What then was

behind the urgency of the build-up?

The answer to this question lies in an understanding of how the build-up would have altered NATO's function:

A build-up of ground forces on even a lesser scale [than planned] . . . began to provide a somewhat new conception of NATO's military meaning. Europe's ground forces might not be able alone to meet and defeat a fully mobilized ground attack by the Soviet Union; but, on the other hand, NATO was clearly a force *which could obstruct a march from East Germany to the Channel.* [Emphasis added.]

One corollary of NATO's new meaning would be to preclude the Soviet's use of its deterrent, i.e. occupation of Western European cities, and would therefore make Russia vulnerable to nuclear attack. This change in NATO's military meaning, thus was well tailored to fit in with plans for creating a situation of strength in which the Soviet Union could be served with an ultimatum. . . .

In sum, far from being responsive in character or directed towards *negotiating* a settlement which would end the division of Europe and the cold war, U.S. post-war policies of containment and of creating situations of strength were designed, basically, to translate an existing military and economic *superiority* of power into an absolute *supremacy* of power, meaning the ability to dictate terms to the Soviet Union.

IV. THE CREATION OF AN INTEGRATED MILITARY FORCE

George C. Marshall: AMERICAN TROOPS FOR A NATO ARMY

During the Korean War, General Marshall, Secretary of Defense, urged the Senate of the United States to authorize the sending of ground troops to Europe as a means of deterring possible Russian aggression in that area while we were distracted by the conflict in Korea. He also urged the Senate to support the principle of a unified defense command in order to give the North Atlantic Community an integrated military establishment.

STATEMENT OF HON. GEORGE C. MARSHALL, SECRETARY OF DEFENSE

SECRETARY MARSHALL. Mr. Chairman, I have a prepared statement to read, and I will then try to answer the questions that you may see fit to ask me.

The Chairman. Very well.

During this hearing, I hope everyone will be quiet and preserve order. It is the only way we can transact business. We cannot run a horse show here.

Secretary Marshall. In regard to the question under consideration this morning, it seems to me that fundamentally the real issue is what should we do, the United States, in our own self-interest as a nation.

Whatever we do in the way of giving military assistance to Western Europe naturally requires the wholehearted support of the Nation. The trouble seems to be somewhat a state of confusion in the public mind, and for evident reasons, as to just what the situation is and, more specifically, what are the military necessities.

DEVELOPMENT OF NORTH ATLANTIC DEFENSE

In one sense, this is not a new issue for you gentlemen to be discussing in this room, because many of you considered much the same issue when the Senate Foreign Relations Committee was considering the Vandenberg resolution, S. R. 239, of the Eightieth Congress.

Much the same issue also was before you a few months earlier when I was called to testify here in support of the European recovery program.

The action of the Senate in 1949 when it voted 82 to 13 in favor of the North Atlantic Treaty, and then 55 to 24 in favor of the military-aid program was, I took it to be, a confirmation of the view that the independence of the North Atlantic community of nations was of vital importance not only to the further development of free and democratic governments but also to the security of this country. To be more specific, in enacting the military-aid program, your commit-

From George C. Marshall, "Assignment of Ground Forces of the United States to Duty in the European Area," *Hearings, 82nd Congress, 1st Session* (Washington: U. S. Government Printing Office, 1951), pp. 38–42.

49

tee added to the basic legislation a re-
quirement that the bulk of the funds to
carry out the program would not be
available until there had been prepared
and then approved by the President integrated plans for the defense of the
North Atlantic area.

Since then there have been five meetings of the Defense Ministers of the
North Atlantic Treaty nations, at the
fourth of which I presided. In addition,
there have been numerous meetings of
the Military Committee in which General Bradley represented the United
States and a number of meetings of the
North Atlantic Council at which the Secretary of State represented the United
States. Further, the Standing Group,
consisting of one representative from the
United Kingdom, one from France, and
one from the United States — General
Bradley representing this country — has
been in almost daily session.

Out of all these meetings has emerged,
as Congress expressly stipulated, a plan
for the integrated defense of the North
Atlantic area — a plan which will succeed or will fail, depending upon two
fundamental factors: First, the support
which it receives from this country and
the other nations associated with us; and,
second, the ability with which it is carried out by General Eisenhower and the
staff he is now assembling. Regarding
the second point, I am sure I am right in
the belief that none of you have any misgivings. It is the first point to which
your deliberations here appear to be addressed.

HOW CAN NORTH ATLANTIC COMMUNITY BEST BE PROTECTED?

Please permit me to state the issue as
I see it, in a rather different form. I assume that no one will differ from my
belief that the United States will be

safer — that is, more secure — if governments friendly to the United States are
in power throughout the North Atlantic
community. If this is correct, the question then resolves itself into the problem
of how the nations of the North Atlantic
community can best protect their independence. This is the problem to which
all of our discussions under that treaty
have been addressed.

In my opinion, the course outlined by
our planning is the logical one. We are
building up in the United States and in
each of the nations of the North Atlantic
community stronger armed forces. We
are not building up these stronger forces
for any aggressive purpose, but in order
to enable us to defend ourselves if we
should be attacked. Also, our aim is primarily to deter aggression if that be possible and to defeat aggression if, in spite
of all our efforts, the actions of the Soviet
Union or its satellites should precipitate
another world war.

Fundamental to all of our efforts in
this regard is the immediate start toward
the creation in western Europe of strong
and integrated forces — land, sea, and air
— in such proportions to one another as
appears reasonable and practicable.

UNITED STATES CONTRIBUTION TO INTEGRATED FORCES IN EUROPE

As General Eisenhower pointed out in
recent testimony here, the United States
forces will constitute only a minor portion of these proposed integrated forces
— the major portion being furnished by
the Western European nations. This is
particularly true in the matter of ground
forces. Because of the great amount of
discussion which has been centered on
the subject of ground forces, I have obtained the express permission of the President to discuss with you the specific
strength of the ground forces which the

United States has planned to maintain in Europe in the present emergency.

I take this step reluctantly because of the security considerations involved, but I have reached the conclusion that there is a greater peril to our security through weakening the morale of our allies by a debate based upon uncertainties than there can possibly be through the public disclosure of our planned-strength figures.

I will reread that paragraph: I take this step reluctantly because of the security considerations involved, but I have reached the conclusion that there is a greater peril to our security through weakening the morale of our allies by a debate based upon uncertainties than there can possibly be through the public disclosure of our planned-strength figures.

SIX UNITED STATES DIVISIONS TO BE IN EUROPE

To be specific, the Joint Chiefs of Staff have recommended to me, and I have so recommended to the President — and the President has approved — a policy with respect to our forces in Europe which looks to the maintenance by us, in Europe, of approximately six divisions of ground forces.

We already have there, on occupation duty, about two divisions of ground forces. Our plans, based on the recommendation of the Joint Chiefs of Staff, therefore contemplate sending four additional divisions to Europe.

While this number does not appear to represent in pure fighting strength a large contribution to the immediate defensive strength of Western Europe, it does represent a small Army unit of high efficiency, and we believe a tremendous morale contribution to the effectiveness and build-up of the projected ground

forces the North Atlantic Treaty nations are undertaking to develop under General Eisenhower's direction and command.

OUR FRIENDS MUST CONTRIBUTE FULLY

As President Truman pointed out in his announcement on September 9, 1950 —

The basic element in the implementation of this decision is the degree to which our friends match our actions in this regard. Firm programs for the development of their forces will be expected to keep full step with dispatch of additional United States forces to Europe.

General Eisenhower outlined to you the responsibility which he possesses, and which he intends to exercise, to assure that all members of the North Atlantic Treaty contribute the maximum amount of strength which their geographic, economic, and manpower situations permit. In the key position to which he has been named at the request of the nations which make up the North Atlantic Treaty Organization, General Eisenhower will be in a position to insist that all members of the North Atlantic Treaty play their full parts in this vital undertaking.

AMERICAN AIR AND NAVAL CONTRIBUTIONS

Proportionately, the American contribution will be greater in air and in naval forces than in ground forces, for the greater strength of the United States is in the air and on the sea. Proportionately also, our contribution will be greater in the production of munitions than in the provision of manpower, for the industrial capacity of the United States is the greatest of any of the member nations of the North Atlantic Treaty.

In all that we are doing, as just outlined, we are specifically carrying out the instructions of the Congress with respect to the preparation, and the approval by the President, of integrated plans for the defense of the North Atlantic area. As a result of the various steps outlined earlier these plans are now well advanced, and General Eisenhower as you know, has assumed supreme command.

FREEDOM OF ACTION FOR GENERAL EISENHOWER

In order for him to succeed in this most difficult and critical of assignments, it is essential that he not be deprived of that freedom of action which is so necessary to a military commander. I realize, of course, that whenever this issue of flexibility is raised, some people will say, "If the fighting starts in Europe, the military commanders will be given complete freedom of action."

But what we want above everything else is something infinitely more important — namely, a certain freedom of action to establish a deterrent against the development of a general war.

Moving in an international setting in a military way is at best fraught with many and often great difficulties. We had them throughout the last world war but we successfully overcame the problems and proceeded to a victorious conclusion of the war. In this situation though, we have a far more delicate and more dangerous situation to deal with. The most important, the greatest factor in the creation of military strength for Western Europe in my opinion is to build up morale — of the will to defend — the determination to fight if that be necessary. And because of the events of the past few years and the increasing threat presented by the Soviet Union, we have an exceedingly difficult situation with which to deal, in the way of preparations which we hope will enable us to avoid war and will help us to take the necessary action if war is thrust upon us. Under these conditions, having in mind the various measures which have been taken by the Senate in regard to the North Atlantic community, the fewer limitations you impose upon the Military Establishment the better off we will be. And, incidentally, I would say, gentlemen, that it is not a question today of having large bodies of troops ready to march down to the docks and embark for Europe. Our problem is the creation of troops. The limiting factor today, by far the most critical factor, is the long time yet required to do this.

Those of you who are members of the Armed Services Committee have been addressing yourselves to this problem for many weeks and I will therefore not repeat here what we are doing to achieve this build-up as rapidly as possible.

Robert E. Osgood: REARMAMENT AND RELAXATION

Robert E. Osgood, professor at the School of Advanced International Studies of The Johns Hopkins University, observed the effects upon the Atlantic Alliance of the Soviet explosion of an atomic device in 1949 and of the outbreak of the Korean conflict. Although structural changes were forced on NATO, Osgood noted that conflicting goals among the

Reprinted from NATO: The Entangling Alliance, pp. 74–87, by Robert Endicott Osgood by permission of The University of Chicago Press. © 1962 by The University of Chicago.

allies nullified most of the prospects for an integrated military force. Nevertheless such changes as were made did advance the "common interest in securing America's commitment and material support."

NEW COMPLICATIONS AND THE BEGINNING OF RELAXATION

THE outbreak of the Korean War completed the transformation of NATO from a multilateral guaranty pact into a semi-integrated military organization designed to redress the military imbalance on the Continent. At the same time, it destroyed the original balance of assets and liabilities for the major allies and drastically altered the original distribution of burdens and benefits, while complicating the task of strategic collaboration.

In seeking new terms of collaboration that would be compatible with the higher level of allied commitments and contributions, the United States, soon after the invasion of Korea, increased her military assistance to the European allies, assumed the central military command of NATO, and promised to place additional American troops on the Continent, while the European allies agreed to put rearmament and the build-up of NATO forces ahead of economic advancement and, in principle, accepted West German participation in the common defense.

In the aftermath of the Korean scare, these new terms of collaboration increased NATO's military strength enough to restore allied confidence in the stability of deterrence against overt military aggression upon Western Europe, but they failed to elicit sufficient contributions to meet the pledged force levels, which the allies had agreed were essential to defend Western Europe if deterrence should fail. Yet, although the alliance had undertaken a military effort that exceeded the willingness of its mem-

bers to execute, it could not revert to its original form without disrupting the whole enterprise. Therefore, although the gap between strategy and capabilities was somewhat narrowed, the disparity between the pledged and the actual contributions to NATO was greatly enlarged. Now the United States, having firmly committed herself to close the gap between strategy and capabilities, once more assumed the task of inducing her allies — again, with inadequate concessions and sanctions — to fulfil their pledged contributions to collective defense.

At the same time, in the period between the outbreak of the Korean War and NATO's adoption in December, 1954, of a new strategy relying upon tactical nuclear weapons, there arose new political, economic, and military developments to complicate the requirements of allied security and collaboration: the Soviet "relaxation of tensions," the intensification of allied involvements outside the NATO area, the economic strain of rearmament, and the American and Russian achievements of hydrogen explosions. These developments simultaneously increased the hazards of depending upon America's strategic nuclear striking power and reduced allied incentives to build the ground power that might mitigate this dependence.

The decisive factor underlying all NATO's new problems of security and collaboration was the rapid decline of the fear of aggression, which had led NATO to rearm. When it appeared that the Korean War was a limited war confined to the Korean peninsula and not

the prelude to other aggressions insti-
gated by the Soviet Union, the fear of
imminent aggression in Europe quickly
gave way to the fear that the United
States might either precipitate a world
war or else become so fascinated by the
Chinese Communist threat in the Far
East as to neglect her European commitments. The long period of stalemate and
truce in Korea, starting in the spring and
summer of 1951, sapped all sense of
urgency.

Prime Minister Churchill, upon assuming office after the defeat of the Labor
government, a defeat which was in no
small part due to its responsibility for the
Korean-inspired rearmament program,
expressed the general revival of confidence in the efficacy of deterrence:

Looking back over the last few days, I
cannot feel that the danger of a third world
war is so great now as it was at the time of
the Berlin Air Lift crisis in 1948, when the
Labor Government . . . took great risks in a
firm and resolute manner. Of course, no
one can predict the future, but our feeling,
on assuming responsibility, is that the deterrents have increased and that, as the deterrents have increased, the danger has become
more unlikely.

John Foster Dulles, speaking as the
prospective Republican Secretary of
State early in the presidential campaign
of 1952, returned to his pre-Korean estimate of the Soviet military threat, "When
we analyze the Soviet military threat," he
said, "we can find many reasons to believe that it may not be more than an un-
used threat, designed partly for defense
but chiefly to throw the free world into
panic." Disputing the view that the
Soviet leaders relied upon overt military
force as a means of conquest, he asked
why, if this were so, they had not attacked in Europe or Asia, where they
would meet no "appreciable opposition,"

and why they should wait until the West
built up its defenses. "One reason," he
answered,

is that the Communist leaders of Russia are
almost as afraid of the Red Army as we are.
. . . A second reason is the supreme skill of
the political leaders of Russia in the art of
political warfare. A third reason may be that
which Mr. Churchill has several times suggested, namely, that they fear the striking
power of our atomic weapons.

Both of these estimates of Soviet intentions were the basis, in their respective countries, upon which incoming governments reduced defense expenditures
and ground force goals on the supposi-
tion that concentration upon strategic
airpower would provide more security at
a tolerable cost. Throughout Europe,
similar estimates assured the restoration
of domestic economic priorities over rearmament. To be sure, the European
allies — France, in particular — continued
to seek and to receive American assurances that NATO was pledged to defend
their territories in the event of aggression, but they were impelled more by a
desire to satisfy domestic criticisms and
suspicions of the alliance than by an
active fear of invasion. Feeling incapable of redressing the Continental balance of power by themselves, they were
content to rely upon America's atomic
might and her immense industrial and
military potential to deter aggression and
to let the United States, who had the
most direct interest in counterbalancing
Soviet power, worry about enlarging the
ground forces. In the meanwhile, they
were more impressed by the burden of
rearmament than by the danger of aggression.

AMERICAN TROOPS FOR EUROPE

The most important concessions that
the United States made as a stimulant to

allied rearmament were the appointment of General Eisenhower as Supreme Commander of the NATO forces in Europe and the placement of four more American divisions (making a total of almost six) on the forward line in West Germany. But once these concessions were made, they provided little inducement to further European efforts, while the threat to withdraw them proved worse than useless as a sanction, since these visible symbols of the American commitment came to be regarded as the prerequisites of allied military collaboration.

However, the fundamental obstacle to a vast build-up of NATO forces was not the weakness of American concessions or sanctions but the fact that the announced strategic objectives of the build-up were not sufficiently compelling to warrant the effort. In fact, the same lack of strategic inducement to enlarging ground forces was conspicuous in the defense policies of the United States, who could far better afford the effort. In spite of the greater sense of urgency about rearmament in the American government, the debate over sending additional troops to Europe showed that Americans were no more inclined to adjust their national strategy and capabilities to a conception of massive land warfare than were Western Europeans. Yet, for less ambitious objectives, a much more modest build-up seemed sufficient.

When the Eighty-second Congress convened in January, 1951, Senator Taft reopened a lengthy debate on President Truman's announced intention to send troops to Europe. Taft did not oppose sending a few American divisions to Europe to help the Europeans build up their armies, providing that they made a sufficient effort of their own. What he objected to was committing the United States to fight the world-wide battle of communism "primarily on the vast

land areas of the continent of Europe or the continent of Asia, where we are at the greatest disadvantage in a war with Russia." America's proper strategic role, he insisted, was to provide air and sea power, while the Eurasian countries provided the troops. But, with or without American aid, he could not foresee Europe providing enough troops to withstand a Russian attack. The effort would not only be futile but provocative. This theme was reiterated by Herbert Hoover, Senator Wherry, and other opponents of the President's policy.

Supporters of the President's policy relied heavily upon the persuasiveness of General Eisenhower, who returned from Europe in February in order to testify in its behalf. Yet Eisenhower's testimony fell far short of indorsing the strategic conception Taft criticized. In fact, in some respects it was more like an indorsement of Taft's position. Thus, the Supreme Commander emphasized the contribution of American troops to European morale not to creating a Continental ground force.

What we are trying to do, ladies and gentlemen, is to start a sort of reciprocal action across the Atlantic. We do one thing which inspires our friends to do something, and that gives us greater confidence in their thoroughness, their readiness for sacrifice. We do something more and we establish an upward-going spiral which meets this problem of strength and morale.

America's role in this enterprise, he said, was to serve as a center of production and inspiration but not as a supplier of troops to the various critical sectors around the vast Sino-Soviet bastion in Eurasia. "Our view in the central position must be directed to many sectors," he said.

We cannot concentrate all our forces in any one sector, even one as important as

Western Europe. We must largely sit here with great, mobile, powerful reserves ready to support our policies, our rights, our interests wherever they may be in danger in the world.

When Secretary of Defense Marshall revealed that the United States intended to send no more than four divisions to Europe, this virtually eliminated the immediate issue of America's role in NATO's build-up, but it did not meet the underlying issue of the strategic objective which the build-up was intended to support. Secretary of State Acheson gave the most lucid explanation of NATO's strategy, but the strategic objectives that he emphasized neither required nor inspired the construction of the huge standing army that military plans had specified since pre-NATO days. He said that the first purpose of NATO's forces in Europe was to deter aggression and that, in order to deter aggression, reliance upon retaliatory airpower was not enough. The reason he gave for this conclusion followed the reasoning of NSC 68.

One reason why we cannot continue to rely on retaliatory air power as a sufficient deterrent is the effect of time. We have a substantial lead in air power and in atomic weapons. At the present moment, this may be the most powerful deterrent against aggression. But with the passage of time, even though we continue our advances in this field, the value of our lead diminishes. In other words, the best use we can make of our present advantage in retaliatory air power, is to move ahead under this protective shield to build the balanced collective forces in Western Europe that will continue to deter aggression after our atomic advantage has been diminished.

Here was, perhaps, the earliest official public statement of the strategic implica-

tions of Russia's capacity to neutralize the deterrent effect of America's nuclear striking power, but, pleading security reasons, Acheson declined to elaborate. Moreover, he left somewhat ambiguous the precise strategic conclusion to be drawn from his analysis. If more ground forces were needed to compensate for the declining deterrent power of the Strategic Air Command, what kind of contingencies would they be designed to deter? Here Acheson reiterated his earlier statement of the function of ground forces in deterring limited aggression. He foresaw the possibility not only of indirect aggressions on the Czechoslovakian model but also of direct military incursions by Soviet satellites, which the Soviet Union could disclaim; and he warned that, "in the absence of defense forces-in-being, satellites might be used for such disguised aggression in the hope that they could get away with it, since the free nations could respond only with the weapons of all-out general war, or not at all."

But if the ground forces were intended only to deter limited *fait accompli*'s, this would not require building up an army capable of stopping a major Soviet assault on the ground. Should NATO abandon this more ambitious strategic objective? Acheson indicated that it should not. The first purpose of ground forces, he said, was to deter limited and major aggressions, but, if the deterrent failed and Russia launched an all-out assault, the ground forces would have to hold air bases and detain the attack long enough to permit airpower to stem the invasion by striking at the aggressor's homeland before he could consolidate control of the great war potential of Western Europe. Apparently, ground forces were expected to perform the same protective function in a bilateral as in a unilateral nuclear war. "These are the forces," Acheson declared, "that would prevent Europe, in the event of an attack, from having to go through another occupation and liberation."

The European allies might be willing to build a force capable of deterring limited aggression, but would they build a force large enough to prevent Europe from being overrun, especially when they could expect even an unoccupied Europe to be devastated by a Soviet-American nuclear exchange? Everyone avoided a direct answer to this troublesome question. Acheson simply denied any intention of matching the potential aggressor "man for man" or "tank for tank." General J. Lawton Collins, chief of staff of the Army, vigorously denied that Europe need be overrun by an all-out assault, but he did not designate the size of the forces that would be required to protect Europe. However, General Eisenhower, who was urging a rapid build-up by 1952, said he would have to see 40 divisions before he would "feel better"; and he looked forward to 60 fully equipped divisions by 1954.

There is no reason to think that the military planners had abandoned their view that a force approaching 100 divisions would be necessary to withstand a Soviet invasion. Yet in 1951 it was already obvious that only the fear of imminent invasion, and certainly not the temporary placement of six American divisions on the Continent, could conceivably inspire the Europeans to make sufficient contributions of men, money, and equipment to support a strategic objective which the United States herself expected to support primarily with airpower. On the other hand, NATO did seem to be making satisfactory progress toward achieving co-ordinated ground forces, airfields, and a network of supporting communications and supplies, which would be sufficient to support the strategic objective Acheson had emphasized: the deterrence of local *fait accompli*'s. In the aftermath of the Korean scare, Europe's growing confidence in its achievement of this modest deterrent capability sapped the only compelling military incentive for enlarging NATO's standing army.

ECONOMIC AND POLITICAL OBSTACLES TO REARMAMENT

While the incentives for expanding allied forces sharply declined, the incentives for cutting back the whole post-Korea defense effort became overwhelming as the strains of rearmament aggravated economic problems and political discontent in the NATO countries. In spite of a general increase in the production and trade of Western Europe, the rearmament program caused a steep rise in the price of imported raw materials in relation to a slower rise in the price of manufactured exports and thereby created balance-of-payments deficits, especially in Great Britain. Concomitant with the balance-of-payments crisis there was a renewal of inflation in the prices of raw materials and foodstuffs in both exporting and importing countries, which, in turn, led Western European governments to pare expenditures for civilian consumption and, in some cases, to impose rationing and price and wage controls, if only to be able to finance rearmament.

These economic repercussions created domestic political problems that were especially galling for governments that had committed themselves to extensive social welfare programs, which now seemed threatened by arms expenditures. On May 15, 1951, French Defense Minister Jules Moch was ejected from the Socialist party's national executive committee for emphasizing the need to sacrifice certain social security benefits for the sake of defense requirements. On September 18, the Netherlands' Foreign Minister, Dr. Dirk U. Stikker, warned the North Atlantic Council that "any further lowering of the present living standard in Europe without the prospect of a rise in the near future will endanger the social peace on the home front which is so essential to our defense effort."

In England the Labor government's arms program, which was expected to cost about 14 per cent of the national income, led Minister of Labor Aneurin Bevan and two of his followers to resign from the government in protest. He and his supporters gave voice to views that were widely shared by politicians in both parties, who hesitated to state them so boldly. They charged that neither England nor the other allied states in Europe could finance rearmament programs of the proposed scale and pace and at the same time maintain their programs for increasing civilian production, building homes, and improving social services. They held that Great Britain, in particular, suffered from carrying a disproportionate share of the West's defense effort, which afforded the United States and other allies a competitive advantage in industrial production and prevented Britain from manufacturing and selling enough export goods to solve its international balance-of-payments problem. Furthermore, they denied the basic strategic premise of rearmament in asserting that the real and sufficient deterrent of aggression in Europe was the American guaranty and not ground forces, while they condemned the American-sponsored build-up as provocative. The victory of the Bevanites and the defeat of the Labor party in the general elections of October, 1951, forcefully demonstrated the political hazards of rearmament.

Against these formidable economic and political obstacles the United States assumed the task of urging her allies to maintain the priority of rearmament over economic advancement in order to create as many battle-ready divisions as possible by 1952, but the European allies responded by beseeching the United States to direct as much foreign aid as possible toward meeting their economic problems in order to mitigate the strains of rearmament. As a French official explained to an American reporter,

With you Americans the big problem is the immediate threat of Russia to our collective security. With us the big problem is the immediate threat to standards of living which cannot be depressed materially without endangering public support for the rearmament program you are demanding of us.

The result of this divergence of interests was that the allies made just enough paper concessions to the build-up of ground forces to sustain America's attachment to NATO, while the United States agreed, in principle, that the build-up should not be made at the sacrifice of national standards of living.

At the Rome meeting of the North Atlantic Council, in November, 1951, the allied powers resolved to create a NATO ground force of 43 divisions by 1954 and to accelerate the "short-term" (1952) program of rearmament, subject to the findings of a twelve-nation Temporary Council Committee, which had been charged with determining the defense expenditures that the respective allies were economically capable of contributing to the collective effort. However, the draft report of a working group (the "Three Wise Men"), which was submitted to the TCC in December, proposed levels of expenditure that obviously exceeded the political, if not the economic, capabilities of the allied governments. And the specific distribution of the economic burden among the allies was as disturbing as the magnitude of the assessments. The report urged the European allies to expand production by an average of 14 per cent by June, 1954, and to increase military expenditures by from 5 per cent for France to 50 per cent for Belgium. It assured them that these goals could be achieved without increasing taxation or reducing standards of living, and it suggested that the way to accomplish this feat was for Western Europe to pay for rearmament out of increased production and for the United States to buy more defense supplies abroad. These ambitious recommendations quickly proved to be unrealistic in terms of the willingness of the allies either to subordinate domestic to defense considerations or to subordinate national defense programs to a supranational determination of burden-sharing.

Although the TCC was supposed to indicate to the European allies how they should close the gap between military needs and actual capabilities by their own efforts, it was clear to all the assembled finance ministers that the essential component in the recommended prescriptions for reconciling rearmament with domestic economic goals would have to be a substantial increase in American assistance. Yet the United States secretary of the treasury had already advised the Rome meeting that Europe could not expect increased American aid for defense programs, and the American Congress had reduced the government's requested funds for the Mutual Security Act, cutting most deeply into the appropriations for economic aid for Europe. This tendency to reduce the total Mutual Security Act appropriation for Europe and allocate a greater proportion to military as opposed to economic aid was carried out in the requests

and authorizations for fiscal year 1953.

Furthermore, the United States secretary of defense had let the European governments know that the American government intended to pare down its own defense budget (with the exception of airpower) for the sake of the stability of the national economy. And Congress subsequently approved this policy by cutting the administration's total defense budget (although granting generous appropriations to the Air Force, which it had consistently urged the administration to expand). Thus, even while the United States reduced the military and economic assistance that the allied powers in Europe needed in order to fulfil their rearmament pledges without sacrificing their economic and social goals, she provided them, in her own defense policies, with the irresistible formula for squaring economic retrenchment with national security.

THE QUESTION OF GERMAN PARTICIPATION
IN WESTERN DEFENSE

Before the North Atlantic allies convened in Lisbon in February, 1952, in order to agree upon the force levels required to implement the American-sponsored rearmament program, the United States also encountered allied resistance in pushing another logical concomitant of NATO's forward strategy: the participation of West Germany in the European security system.

In September, 1950, the State Department had proposed incorporating about ten German divisions directly under NATO command. But throughout Western Europe, and especially in France, strong opposition had developed to rushing ahead with German rearmament and membership in NATO before political safeguards against German militarism had been created.

In order to postpone German participation the French Premier, René Pleven, put forward a counterproposal, analogous to the "Schuman Plan" for economic integration through a European Coal and Steel Community. This scheme would so tightly integrate Germany's military contribution in a European framework — chiefly by confining German units to combat teams within international divisions of a European army — as to obviate the danger of independent national action. The "Pleven Plan" was widely regarded as a politically impossible and militarily unfeasible subterfuge for preventing German rearmament. Nevertheless, the United States, after first rejecting the scheme as unrealistic and unfeasible, later indorsed it in order to gain French adherence to a German contribution. She indorsed it, however, in the altered form of a European Defense Community, which would include German divisions integrated on a basis of equality with other national divisions in army groups.

Thus, the French trapped themselves and their allies into accepting, in principle, a European army with supranational features, which it is doubtful that even the United States would have accepted in fact. Yet only the American government regarded EDC as an urgent military necessity, and only the West German government took a keen political interest in the project.

In France the proponents of EDC in the long, intricate debate in the National Assembly argued for the scheme primarily as a means of tying down American troops in Europe, restraining the resurgent Federal Republic within a Franco-German rapprochement, and promoting the grand scheme of European reconstruction through unification. Both sides of the argument displayed almost total indifference to strategic military considerations.

In England the support of EDC as an assurance against American isolation — and as a means of getting Germany to share the burdens of rearmament and compete on more equal terms with British trade — held an uneasy balance over the fear of German ascendance on the Continent and the traditional British opposition to becoming involved in European commitments. But, as in France, the general disposition of proponents and opponents alike was to let America's nuclear power take care of NATO's military security.

In West Germany, Chancellor Adenauer's government, against great popular and political opposition to rearmament, embraced the idea of integrating German troops in a European army — providing they were under national control — as a means of abolishing the restrictions of the Occupation Statute, restoring Germany to equal status among the major powers, laying the ancient ghost of Franco-German hostility, and interlocking Germany's destiny with that of the Western world; in short, for the sake of the larger purpose of restoring German power and prestige within an international framework that would protect Germany and her neighbors from the revival of German chauvinism. But neither inside nor outside the government was there any significant appreciation of, nor concern for, the military implications of EDC.

Thus, on the eve of NATO's adoption of the most ambitious defense program in its history, the two major contributions to this program — rearmament and the participation of West Germany — depended upon the convergence of the contributing nations' disparate political aims and their common interest in securing America's commitment and material support, rather than upon educated convictions about the military requirements of common defense. It is little wonder, then, that the large force goals indorsed at Lisbon turned out to be paper promises. Yet the rearmament effort, which was built upon those goals, eventually led to two other results that were no less important for European security and cohesion: the membership of West Germany in NATO and the further commitment of the United States and Britain to the defense of Continental Europe.

Theodore H. White: THE BASIN OF FREEDOM

Theodore H. White has made a distinguished reputation as a writer and journalist in several areas of international and national concern. In the early 1950's he served as a correspondent for The Reporter *in Western Europe. In* Fire in the Ashes *(1953), he voiced his optimism about the future of Europe and credited much of its new confidence to the role NATO played in defending Europe from potential attack.*

IN politics, those things we cannot see are always more important than those we can. This is because the most stubborn and important facts are ideas that exist in people's minds and not the way those ideas express themselves in guns and concrete, buildings and roads. This is why the biggest political fact in the Western world is the most difficult to describe.

The name of this idea is a dull alphabetical label, NATO, an addition of four initials which stand for the North Atlantic Treaty Organization.

Much of NATO is, to be sure, hard, tactile and visible, showing itself in a thousand faces. Just six miles outside of Paris the western speedway of St. Cloud throws off a dark ribbon of cobblestone that deposits you before a gray building called SHAPE, outside which snap the flags of fourteen nations in brilliant reds, golds, blue, whites, greens. This is part of NATO. But NATO is also six noncoms in the early hours of the morning, monitoring spitting radios and clicking teletype machines in one room that centralizes a web of invisible lines that make the Atlantic Basin, from Washington to Istanbul, from the North Cape to Sicily, one net of instant communication. NATO is an airfield in northern France with the pilots of six nations scrambling into the air, flying French, British, American jets, listening to the command of an Englishman who takes orders from a Belgian who is under control of an American, and all getting up to combat height within two minutes to attack the imaginary enemy. It is also a white, hushed building on a hill above the Seine, carpeted with thick brown felt where permanent delegates of 14 nations, supported by an international staff of 150 economists, soldiers and diplomats sit in constant session, totting up the plans and powers of 365,000,000 people. . . . NATO is the Reception Hall of the Elysée Palace with the red and blue uniformed chamber orchestra of the Garde Republicaine playing Mozart under the glistening chandeliers beneath Gobelin tapestries, while all the great men of the West — Edens and Schumans, Plevens and de Gasperis, Ridgways, Alexanders, Achesons, Harrimans, Wilsons, Butlers — stalk about sipping champagne and nibbling petits fours from the flower-burdened buffet tables. But it is also the windswept bridge of an American aircraft carrier operating at night in the North Sea with a polyglot screen of foreign destroyers in front of it; the admiral orders the screen to close up in combat pattern ahead of him, and on the radarscope he can see the luminous pips turn slowly and fall precisely into combat pattern. "And," says the admiral later, "do you know it wasn't until morning that I could look out and tell what nationality they were, but they were all right there in place during the night."

NATO is all this — but these are only its outer faces. At its heart NATO is an idea, an idea which has taken years to flesh out into the imposing fact of its present dominance in world politics. This idea is that somehow, in a way no one can quite describe, there grew up about the Atlantic Basin a civilization which is like no other in the world. In this civilization the individual man and liberty are the measure of political value. Together the people on both sides of this great ocean (less than a sixth of the population of the world) makes a community in the greatest sense, bred out of traditions, religions and technology that none of the other major civilizations of the world share. It has taken centuries of internecine bloodshed to make them realize that they are one. Not until now, when desperately challenged by other counterattacking civilizations, have the men who live around the Atlantic realized that they must band themselves together to defend, each people with its lives and substance, the lives and substance of

every other member. It is an alliance like no other in history, for at its base lie no objectives of spoil or conquest. All the rest of the globe may be bargained over, but NATO itself was not erected for bargaining. It was erected for defense of the heartland of freedom and a heritage which only too late was realized to be common property. It is within NATO that America finally came of age in world affairs, pledging herself for the first time, by a revolutionary act of statesmanship, to sacrifice men and treasure not at her own will and timing but whenever any member of the Community of the Atlantic should be wantonly attacked. . . .

NATO began in the spring of 1949 in a total fog in which there twirled in absolute confusion a number of imposing committees that circulated like roadshows between Paris, London, Washington. In this fog, lesser committees of soldiers, known as Regional Planning Groups, measured off the various sectors of defense, assigned them, north, south, and central. Each little committee assumed that all the might of the Red Army would come to bear on its sector alone, and so calculating, they all made their requests for troops. When added together their demands reached the total of 307 divisions for Europe alone, or something like three times the Allied strength at the height of World War II. Meanwhile, the committees of Finance Ministers, Foreign Ministers and Defense Ministers who are the governing bodies of the Atlantic Community had continued in their blithe assumption that the American war surplus stocks would be sufficient to arm the entire defense effort, with perhaps an extra injection of five billion dollars of American aid to prod the project ahead. NATO's first shock came when the confrontation of civilians and military showed that the gap between the soldiers' demand and civilian provision was of the order of 200 billion dollars. Ever since, the story of NATO, year by year, has been the slow whittling down of the soldiers' estimates of divisions needed for Western defense from 307 to 96 and 70 to 60, and the subordination of their estimates to what the Community can afford to pay.

The present common-sense approach of NATO to its complicated problems was not conceived at any single meeting, at any single conference, by any single decision. A series of jolts propelled NATO from its early madness of irresponsible committees into an organization which now, however primitive, points to the way ahead.

The first series of jolts came to a climax at the Brussels conference of NATO in December of 1950 when, in the first panic of the Korean War, as American troops were flung back in disorder by China's Communist armies, it was recognized finally that committees could not conduct battles. It was then that all the Regional Planning Groups were abolished, that a single military headquarters, SHAPE, was set up with a chain of command over all Atlantic troops on the Continent, that the target of effort was boiled down from 307 divisions to 96 and General Dwight D. Eisenhower, a flesh and blood individual, was named SACEUR, or Supreme Allied Commander Europe.

The second series of jolts climaxed in the Lisbon conference of NATO, early in 1952. Until then, the leadership of NATO had lain in the hands of its soldiers, and chiefly in the magic personality of Dwight D. Eisenhower, with no civilian authority strong enough or wise enough to summon the soldiers to account. At Lisbon, finally, the soldiers were forced to answer to a body of civilians why they wanted the troops they said they needed and to yield to the civilians the decision as to how quickly how much of their request could be met.

At Lisbon, the governments gathered in NATO established a Permanent Council of the North Atlantic Treaty. This Council of fourteen civilians was then housed in Paris to sit in permanent session, supervising the work of the soldiers while constantly communicating with their governments on day-to-day adjustments and problems that rose in the great Alliance.

The Lisbon conference did not so much abolish the end goal of 96 divisions in Western Europe as postpone that goal. The civilians pledged themselves to raise 50 divisions in the following year and agreed to decide future targets only when current targets had been met. (This figure has since been raised, cautiously, in 1953 to a target of 56 ready divisions in Western Europe.) At Lisbon, finally, the old concept of a Soviet timetable of attack and war was set aside. The favorite American date of the year of peril — 1954 — was abandoned. Instead, implicitly, the conferees recognized that perhaps never would there be a showdown year with the Russians, that the Atlantic world was entering into a long period of balancing power with the Communist world and that success or failure would rest on a long-term test of wisdom and equilibrium.

Now, at last, in the year 1953, the Atlantic Community has come to recognize military goals as fluid, changing objectives. For the spring of 1953 marked not only the maturing of SHAPE as a military field command, but also the maturing of two developments long cultivated by the West, yet, until now, too visionary to enter into the hard calculation of combat.

The one is technical — it is our entrance into that era which one of our most eminent American generals has called the era of "atomic plenty." The swift and secret attack by American scientists simultaneously on the problems of nuclear field weapons and of the amazingly accurate NIKE guided missiles came to success only in the fall of 1952. The impact of this success on SHAPE thinking has been profound but is, as yet, immeasurable. Today American generals estimate that three medium bombers could dump the same devastation on a given front as required 2,700 bombers in the breakthrough of Saint Lô in 1944. At SHAPE, all plans and requirements — for field forces, reserves, buildup, composition of tactical air force — are being freshly restudied for the change that must be wrought in them by the addition of these new resources.

The second development which has shaken all SHAPE's previous military calculations is political. This is the startling uprising of the Berlin workers in June of 1953. The Red Army of Occupation in East Germany reacted to the uprising with extraordinary technical efficiency, moving three full divisions into Berlin within twenty-four hours, a feat wringing respect out of professional soldiers no matter what their uniform. But this enormous drain upon an occupation force of only twenty-two divisions, by an unorganized and unsupported uprising of unarmed workers, has revealed a paralyzing weakness at the base of Russian strength. Hitherto, it has been assumed at SHAPE that the Red Army's divisions faced forward, while the policing of Germans in the rear could be handled adequately by the Volks Polizei and Bereitschaften of the Communist East German government. It is now obvious that the East German government cannot guarantee the security of the Red Army's rear, and that the Red Army's twenty-two divisions in Germany (as its eight divisions in the satellites) are insufficient to fight forward and police their rear at the same time. For the first time SHAPE can consider defense strategy in terms of a forward counteroffensive, with support ready and available behind the enemy's lines.

Politically, we live still in what may be called the post-Lisbon transitional era of the Atlantic Community. Twice each year this Community sends its leaders to gather in Paris for the meeting of the North Atlantic — three ministers of state from each of the fourteen members plus planeload after planeload of accompanying experts. Motorcycle escorts screech through Paris as the beflagged limousines purr up the rise to the Palais de Chaillot. The hotels of Paris bristle with strange uniforms as the Military Committee of the Alliance gathers to present the Council with its observations; two-star and three-star generals flick in and out of the Committee rooms bearing bulging brief cases full of top-secret data, dancing attendance like office boys on the yet more imposing four- and five-star generals who will present their thinking to the civilian chieftains sent by the people. For three or four days the ministers sit together studying the report of their military committee, examining the account book of Western Defense, scrutinizing the progress in the field, prying at each other's wills and resistance as they decide what to do next.

Yet these meetings are not nearly as important as the method and understructure of the organization they top. The full council meetings of the great ministers are called only to review and settle the problems that have been refined for them by the Permanent Council, which, with the 150-man corps of international civil servants of NATO's Permanent Secretariat, has sat in year-round supervision and interrogation of parliaments, congresses and soldiers alike. Each summer the soldier staffs of NATO, both at SHAPE and in Washington, start their preparation of next year's military targets — what new airfields they need next, what pilot training programs are required, what divisions must be activated, what support troops must be trained. Simultaneously, NATO's Secretariat has prepared for each member government a questionnaire several inches thick, pressing it for details of performance toward last year's targets, its proposals for expansion and contribution in the coming year, its suggestions for broad NATO development. When all these questionnaires are in, the Secretariat of NATO assembles an over-all picture giving the sum of military effort of all fourteen powers, their weaknesses, their failures in the previous twelve months, their proposed global effort for the coming period. When this civilian compilation has been completed and placed beside the military requirements set by the soldiers at SHAPE, the inevitable gap between military demand and civilian response is apparent, and the ministers of the Atlantic Council have a clear problem to wrestle with.

If this were the only function of the Secretariat they would, of course, be no more than a group of military bookkeepers. But there is much more to their operation. Lightly, almost imperceptibly, NATO's Secretariat has cast an international restraining authority over each nation's sovereign impulses. Long before the ministers gather for political adjustment of their differences, the Secretariat, acting for the Community, has summoned individual powers to account. It has examined the books of a small Scan-

dinavian power and thanked it for its promised increase of one division next year, but persuaded it that, militarily, the Community would prefer to see the increase of strength come not in a divisional formation but in the specialist, supporting troops which SHAPE's generals need for flexibility of action. Long before the soldiers at SHAPE have clearly traced the problems of 1954 and 1955, the Secretariat will have singled out such a problem, say, as spare parts, and pointed out that in another three years, when American deliveries of new equipment to the Alliance cease, the Alliance will break down unless the Europeans, now, create the industries to supply needed spare parts for the American tanks, guns, planes and radar. Simultaneously they point out that this burden of maintenance, added to current military obligations, will by 1955, at the present rate of military growth, equal the outer maximum which economists say Europe can sustain. And what then?

The shadow authority of NATO's Secretariat extends even over the United States, gently intruding in American affairs in a way that only Congress ever exercised before. In September of 1952, for example, the United States replied to NATO's questioning with a 250-page document reporting all our military secrets with the exception of atomic energy and strategic bombing policy. For eleven days, NATO's experts pondered American replies, analyzed them, clarified them by queries to American technicians. Then, still unsatisfied, the Secretariat summoned the Permanent Atlantic Council delegates of the United States to the Palais de Chaillot to answer some twenty points which it considered obscure or confusing.

In the Council room of NATO's headquarters four long tables, covered with the usual green baize cloth, were arranged in a square. At one side sat the American delegates like witnesses in a witness box. Facing them was the secretarial staff of NATO. To their left a table was reserved for other delegates from other nations, for in NATO any nation has the right to sit in judgment on the policy of any other. For the two interrogations of the Americans in 1952, French, British, Italians, Canadians, Danes and Norwegians sent examiners. Then came the questions:

"You say," asked one examiner, "that the United States expects the Korean War to be over by July 1, 1953. Why?"

"You say," asked another expert,

that the United States plans to spend so-and-so much as its contribution to the infrastructure of pipelines, airbases, communications demanded by SHAPE. Do you plan to appropriate it as a separate item or are you going to reduce the foreign aid program pledged to us individually by that amount?

"We asked you," demanded another,

to tell us just how many divisions you have in America available for duty in Europe in time of war and you replied "zero." What does that mean? Does that mean you are going to use the home reserve of American troops independently or that we can expect to have them at SHAPE's command on request?

"How about the answer to that minesweeper question?" asks another.

We asked how many minesweepers America would turn over in a crisis to clear the access channels to Europe and you said "zero." Does that mean you will operate them independently or that you really have none?

"How about America's measures to control inflation?" asked little Denmark,

and was completely dissatisfied with the answer of the giant's spokesman.

To Americans fresh out of home such questions seem like violent intrusions on pride, for no one but American Congressmen have ever had the right to summon the American government to account. Yet NATO's control over America is the gentlest exercised over any government, for all governments must submit to this examination and most are treated more harshly. Only America, when pressed, can infrequently refuse to answer. Only America can consistently hold out, if she wishes, against the infrequent 13-to-1 vote in Council and make it stick. Sometimes the British can resist a 13-to-1 Council vote and occasionally the French, too, dare outface the Alliance. But no smaller power can do else but give in to a 13-to-1 adverse vote; for them NATO is more than a community; it is a new kind of government.

For five years, in Paris, the Communists have cast around for words to smear the effort of the Western world to organize itself. Each word has been chosen by the Communists in an effort to pack the phrase with contempt. Western Europe has been called *les pays colonisés*, or *les pays marshallisés;* the Communists' adversaries have been denounced as "the americanized press," or the "americanized governments"; the process has been deftly ridiculed by calling it the "coca-colonization" of European civilization. Recently, at last, even the Communist press has been wrenched about to use a new word we have forced on it — the word "Atlantic." The policy of the West is now called "the Atlantic policy." This, in a fundamental sense, is a victory, for now communism recognizes a new field of force, a new, if primitive, source of political energy.

It would be pleasant if NATO could

relax now with this force in being and its dearly purchased triumph of military equilibrium in Europe. Yet the Atlantic Community is only at the beginning of a new chapter, probably even more difficult than the old. For it is only by comparing NATO, the governing body of the Atlantic world, with its adversary, the government of the Communist world, that its weaknesses become apparent.

The Russian dictatorship possesses the matchless advantage of being able to deal with an entire family of problems at the same time. The Politburo decision that ordains an army-in-being ordains the factories and resources to provision it; ordains swift turns between peace offensive and malevolence; balances arms, propaganda and resources, between Europe and the Orient, between politics and arms, with a silent shifting of gears. The Russians, globally and politically, are mechanically flexible.

What cramps the Atlantic Powers is lack of flexibility. When the Atlantic Community acts, fourteen different powers must agree at the same time to a common decision. When a startling peril confronts them as did the crises of 1948 and 1950, they can call into being the mighty array of military force that SHAPE now commands. But as each new problem arises in the long balancing contest between the Soviet and the Western world, a new travail must be endured as the fourteen nations attempt to strike a common attitude.

Today, NATO is frozen about the decisions of 1948 and 1950. These decisions rightly saw the Atlantic Basin as the centerpiece in world strategy and moved to secure it; since then, the Atlantic Community has rigidly dedicated itself to the creation and equipment of military divisions in Western Europe. Its success has stimulated new Russian political tactics,

for the Russians react politically as well as strategically; yet NATO, living in its post-Lisbon state, is prepared to cope with none of them.

New problems tumble one upon the other in a cascade that no one is yet prepared to sort out. There are the geographical and political problems of Asia and Germany. The central position of power in the Atlantic is secure, but meanwhile in Asia, in Korea, in Indo-China, in Malaya, the Communists have mounted a vast flanking operation. There can be no strong and healthy France in Europe so long as she is mired and sickened by the infection of war in Indo-China; there can be little even-tempered consideration of policy in America, so long as men die in Korea.

Germany is as difficult a problem as Asia — great as have been its sins, as troublesome as its Occupation has been, its very health has contributed to the revival of Western power. Germany trembles half in, half out, of the Atlantic Community, unable to decide whether, ultimately, to throw its weight with the Community or stand aloof. The larger Atlantic Community cannot be healthy until its leaders have decided on a common attitude to Germany.

The struggle of ideas is equally beyond NATO's present power. NATO possesses body, limbs, organs — but no soul. It keeps books but raises no fresh flags or banners. Its propaganda staff consist of forty-one people (including clerical staff) busy filing press clippings or recording the progress of arms for the world's journals; its entire budget for molding opinion and explaining itself to the world is a trivial $60,000 a year, or one-fifth of the cost of a jet plane. Even more sadly, one must record that no multiplication of budget or personnel would do NATO's public information service any good, for there exists in NATO no central core of thinkers, turning over the ideas of freedom to refresh its dynamic. No serious body of analysis studies the Russians and the Communists in any but military terms, and nothing in NATO provides people with the living image of the free, expanding, fluid society which it is the armies' purpose to guard.

It is here, in political direction, that NATO is sadly wanting. Each nation cautiously shares in NATO a tiny portion of its secret intelligence on the Russians, and the ultimate product is a fuzzy blur in which the enemy's purposes are never seen clearly, and our own purpose frays as a result. British and Americans divide in NATO on the measure of the menace — is it over or is it increasing? Has it ceased to be military and become political, or is it an ever-growing military peril? Americans and French divide violently — do the Russians now plan to upset the economic world in which we live, precipitating us into cycles of depressions, while increasing their own welfare, comfort and economic capacity, as the French hold? Or is their purpose to build and build and build simply to erect a military machine that can crush freedom in one blow, as the Americans hold? All these theses cannot be correct, but if either the British or French or American thesis is the right one, then the Community must take a radical new reading of its purposes in the next few years. Yet it is not prepared to do so, it fumbles while it should decide.

The Atlantic is an area in which people live who are set apart from all other peoples by one underlying concept — that of the free man, his body free from arbitrary arrest, free from arbitrary tax, free to speak, free to gather, free to think. It is this civilization, challenged from within and without, that its member states have joined to protect. Yet they have not even arrived at the definition of their common enmities. Are other peoples with different concepts of life enemies because they are different, or enemies because they are organized by Russian control for potential assault on our homes? Is China an enemy because she is Communist, or is she an enemy because she has become the instrument of Russian diplomacy? Is the civilization of the Middle East dangerous because it wishes to change its relation to the Atlantic Community, or because it flirts with Russian purpose? There are many communities in this coagulating world, only one of which is sworn to destroy Atlantic civilization, the Russian. There are the civilizations of the Moslems, of the Dark Africans, of the Chinese, of the Indians, of Southeast Asians. Toward each, in the new diplomacy of great communities of men, our civilization must have an attitude. Yet NATO is still too confined to consider them.

There remains then a final set of problems: the attitude of NATO'S peoples to each other. NATO's vigor has risen from a military threat, and its directors have rigidly limited their deeds to the legal words of the compact. Therefore, when such a disaster as the floods of the Lowlands desolate the homes of a member country, each member reacts individually shipping sandbags, clothes, medicines to the stricken land, but the great executive machine of the Community, NATO, lies inert, unable to think or act swiftly enough for any other purpose but war. Again, though the European members of NATO recognize that the first upward surge of their recovery is over and that a chill stagnation of industrial expansion has succeeded it, NATO can do nothing. Though NATO was built to erect a barrier behind which the welfare of each nation would increase in peace and safety, it cannot find the authority to examine what next step must be taken to increase that welfare.

The Atlantic Community has, in short, won its first victory — it has created that field of power that finally inspires as Ernest Bevin once hoped "confidence . . . within and respect elsewhere." But this has been a negative victory — it has been a victory of defense, a triumph of resistance. Wars are not won by defense, nor are souls won by men who are simply "against." With the equilibrium of 1953, NATO has arrived only at the end of the beginning. The tasks that knock for admittance to discussion are those of creation, of imagination, of going forward. It is what comes next that counts.

V. DISENGAGEMENT? 1955–1960

George F. Kennan: STRENGTHENING NATO—TO WHAT END?

George F. Kennan retired from the Foreign Service in 1953 to become a member of the Institute for Advanced Studies at Princeton. From this new eminence he continued to study American diplomacy, and had come to the conclusion by 1958 that his containment program had become so rigid as to be unable to respond to new trends in the Soviet Union as well as to changes in Western Europe itself. Because of the expansion of atomic weaponry on both sides of the Iron Curtain a blind military expansion of NATO could lead to mutual destruction. He suggested a return to the Marshall Plan hopes of 1948, when the military role of a future NATO was envisaged as secondary to the construction of a new Europe. He wondered "whether anything has really happened to invalidate this original concept on which both the Marshall Plan and NATO were founded."

WHEN these talks were first conceived some months ago, it was my thought to speak, on this occasion, not of the issues confronting our respective governments at this moment, but of the impact which you in England and we in America have on each other as peoples. I wanted to talk about the similarity of our problems, domestic and foreign; about the foolishness of regarding each other's concerns as something external to ourselves; and about the much greater foolishness of supposing that either of us might stand to gain anything from the reverses and misfortunes of the other. In thinking to talk of these things I had in mind, of course, the unfortunate psychological effects of Suez and other sources of misunderstanding and difference between us.

Today, after four months in England, I find it no longer necessary to speak of these things. A new combination of circumstances and preoccupations has come into being which has made us all feel, I think, that Suez, as an episode, is now very far away indeed.

The heads of our respective governments are at this moment convening in Paris to reaffirm the purposes of the North Atlantic alliance and to see what can be done to make it a stronger instrument for resisting aggression, and everyone senses the extraordinary importance that attaches to their deliberations. It will not be useful now for an outsider to speak of the specific questions they will have before them.

But the occasion is, perhaps, not an unsuitable one for reflecting on the ultimate goal that underlies whatever we do within the framework of NATO. What is it specifically that this organization, and the other Western efforts to meet the Soviet challenge (because NATO is only one of them), are supposed to achieve? To what end are they tending?

To read recent statements of the Soviet

leaders, one would think that the only purpose behind the entire NATO operation was the preparation and eventual unleashing of a preventive war. For years it has been standard propaganda practice in Moscow never to refer to this alliance except as the "aggressive NATO pact."

Now, there may be a few people here and there in the Western countries who would welcome the idea of another war, as a means of dealing with world Communism, and who would think it our business to start it. I cannot recall ever meeting one. Their number, in any case, would scarcely include a single person whose opinion carries weight. The Soviet leaders could make no more useful contribution to the cause of peace, and none that would cost them less, than the abandonment of this absurd and dangerous suggestion. There may be much bewilderment and some real confusion of thought behind the operations of NATO; there may have been statements, here and there, that were subject to misinterpretation. But there is certainly no desire in any responsible Western quarter for another world war, or any intention to unleash one if it can possibly be avoided. If people in Moscow do not already know this, they have ample means for finding it out.

A much more understandable concept of NATO's purpose, though also unsound and incorrect, is that entertained by those who have permitted themselves to view another war as inevitable, either because they expect that the Russians will themselves start it, or because they believe that governments will be carried into it, whether they so desire or not, by the dynamics of political conflict and the weapons race. And, having resigned themselves to the inevitability of war, these people tend to say: let us put aside all other considerations; let us arm to the teeth and with greatest urgency; let us see whether we cannot make our military dispositions such that, when the moment does come, we may at least survive. And it is to NATO that these people naturally look, as one of the major instruments of survival.

Of this view, which ignores the destructiveness of modern weapons and exaggerates the significance of relative changes in military capabilities in this age of nuclear plenty, I have said what I had to say in previous talks. Suffice it to observe here that if the end of our present course were plainly an all-out nuclear war, then any other course would be better.

A third concept of NATO's purpose might be called the cultivation of military strength as a background for an eventual political settlement on our own terms, and without the necessity of compromise. Those who entertain this concept are generally people who have a strong sense of moral righteousness about Western purposes. They believe that once it has been demonstrated to Moscow that successful aggression in Western Europe is not militarily feasible, the Soviet leaders will either appreciate the merit of Western *desiderata* or understand the futility of opposing them, and will retract generally from their present international posture. The West will thus be spared the necessity of compromising its aspirations or of negotiating about matters which as these people see it, are too important in principle to be the subject of negotiation. I hope I do not do too much injustice to the views of these people by this sketchy summary.

This is, from the standpoint of the number and influence of those who entertain it, a much more serious concept than the other I have mentioned. So far as I can see, it has recently had currency in wide and influential circles of Western opinion.

But this view, too, has weaknesses, the recognition of which is vital to the present discussion of NATO policy. It seems to rest, in the first place, on an assumption that Soviet unwillingness to accept Western proposals, particularly the proposals for Europe's future and for general disarmament, arises from the fact that the NATO forces are not as strong as they might be.

I see little evidence for this reasoning. The Soviet reluctance to withdraw from Eastern Germany and to give full freedom to the Eastern European peoples is based partly on political considerations that would not be in any way affected by a stronger NATO, and partly on the existence of precisely that Anglo-American military position on the continent which it is now proposed that we should reinforce.

And it is difficult to believe that a stronger NATO, particularly one that would include missile launching sites on the Continent or the presence of atomic weapons in the arsenals of the continental countries, would increase the inclination of the Soviet Government to accept recent Western disarmament proposals. It might conceivably have this effect if the West were able to offer to withdraw these dispositions as part of an eventual bargain. But elaborate military arrangements of this nature, once put in hand, have consequences. They produce counter measures on the other side. People come to depend on them as essential elements of their security. In the end it becomes difficult to consider their withdrawal or to make them the subject of negotiation. And besides, it is not easy to see what *quid pro quo* Moscow could be expected to extend in the specific matter of atomic weapons in Europe beyond

the offer it has already made to refrain from stationing nuclear weapons in Eastern Germany, Poland and Czechoslovakia. If this offer is not acceptable today, is there reason to suppose it would be more acceptable tomorrow?

I suspect that this view of NATO's purpose, which sees in the alliance a device for avoiding political compromise rather than for facilitating it, rests on these same illusions of relative advantage in the weapons race to which I had occasion to refer in an earlier talk. People think, that is, that if our weapons could only be made a bit stronger than those on the other side, our negotiating position would be just that much better. But if the relative size of the capacity for destruction is becoming increasingly questionable as a military advantage, is it probable that it will have any greater political significance?

How, then, should NATO's purpose be conceived?

When I ask myself this question, my mind goes back to the days in 1948 when the NATO pact was in process of negotiation. I was myself for a time chairman of the working-level subcommittee in which the language of the terms of the pact was thrashed out. Those were hopeful and exciting days. The European Recovery Program, enthusiastically supported on both sides of the water, was then just yielding its first constructive results. There were, of course, even at that time, problems and complications. Europe's economic difficulties were still bitter. The attitude of the Soviet Government was not one whit less disturbing than it is today; on the contrary, Stalin was very much alive, and Moscow was just then preparing the political offensive against Western Europe which later culminated in the Berlin blockade. And if Russia did not yet have atomic weapons, there was no reason to suppose she would not have them, sooner or later.

And yet we were not downhearted, and our eyes were not riveted, as I recall it, on the military balance in Europe, which was actually much less favorable at that time than it is today. I cannot speak here for my friends and colleagues on that subcommittee, but I certainly had no idea at that time that the military instrument we were creating was to be the major vehicle of Western policy in the coming years. It seemed to me that we were setting up a military shield, required less by any imminent actual danger than by the need for a general stabilization of the situation in Europe and for reassurance of the Western European peoples in the light of Soviet military superiority and of their own somewhat traditional and subjective anxieties about land invasion. And behind this shield, I supposed, we would go ahead confidently to meet the Communist danger in its most threatening form — as an internal problem, that is, of Western society; to be combated by reviving economic activity, by restoring the self-confidence of the European peoples, and by helping them to find positive goals for the future.

The Marshall Plan, some of us thought, would be only the beginning: it would lay the foundation for a new sense of purpose in Western society — a sense of purpose needed not just for our protection against an outward threat but to enable us to meet a debt to our own civilization — to become what we ought to be in the light of our traditions and advantages — to accomplish what we would have owed it to ourselves to accomplish, even had such a thing as international Communism never existed. In this vision we saw a new ordering of international relations generally in the Atlantic and European areas, designed

to provide an alternative for peoples who stood at the crossroads in a Europe where the old values had lost their relevance; and it was our hope that this alternative could be made so patently worthy and inspiring in itself, and so wholly without menace to anyone anywhere, that peoples could safely repair to it without raising military issues, without raising questions of great power prestige.

This was the concept around which, outstandingly, the Marshall Plan was built. Only by this means, it seemed to us, could one loosen the great political cramp by which postwar Europe was already beginning to be seized. Only by this means was there any hope that the confused termination of one war could be prevented from growing imperceptibly into the origins of another, and this time one in which all European values would finally perish.

In all of this NATO had, as a military alliance, its part to play; but I think every one of us hoped that its purely military role would decline in importance as the curse of bipolarity fell from the Continent, as negotiations took place, as armies were withdrawn, as the contest of ideologies took other forms. The central agency in this concept was not NATO but the European Recovery Program; and none of us dreamed at that time that the constructive impulses of this enterprise, which looked to everyone so hopeful in those days, would be overtaken and swallowed up in the space of a mere two or three years by programs of military assistance based on a wholly different concept of the Soviet threat and of Europe's needs.

I am not attempting to assign blame for this transformation that has come over the general idea of what we were attempting to accomplish as we approached international Communism. I do not mean to belittle the real changes introduced into our situation by the Soviet acquisition of the nuclear capability and by the appalling advances achieved in the frightfulness of atomic weapons. I do not wish to suggest that the problems faced by our statesmen in this intervening period have been light ones or that the alternatives to this deterioration would have been easy ones to discover and to adopt. Least of all do I mean to absolve the Communists from their share of responsibility for this militarization of thinking about what should never have been regarded at all as a military conflict. Few decisions have ever caused more psychological damage or produced more dangerous confusion than that which started the Korean war in 1950. And this was only one instance of the damage done from the Moscow side.

But I should like to raise today the question whether anything has really happened to invalidate this original concept on which both Marshall Plan and NATO were founded, whether the positive goals of Western policy have really receded so far from the range of practical possibility as to be considered eclipsed by the military danger, whether we would not, in fact, be safer and better off today if we could put our military fixations aside and stake at least a part of our safety on the earnestness of our effort to do the constructive things, the things for which the conditions of our age cry out and for which the stage of our technological progress has fitted us.

Surely everyone, our adversary no less than ourselves, is tired of this blind and sterile competition in the ability to wreak indiscriminate destruction. The danger with which it confronts us is a common danger. The Russians breathe the same atmosphere as we do, they die in the same ways. Problematical as I believe the psychology of the Soviet leaders to be, I cannot warn too strongly against the quick assumption that there is no kernel of sincerity in all these messages with which they have been bombarding the Western chancelleries in recent weeks. Their idea of peace is, of course, not the same as ours. There will be many things we shall have to discuss with them about the meaning of this term before we can agree on very much else. But I see no reason for believing that there are not, even in Moscow's interpretation of this ambiguous word, elements more helpful to us all than the implications of the weapons race in which we are now caught up. And I refuse to believe that there is no way in which we could combine a search for these elements with the pursuit of a reasonable degree of military security in a world where absolute security has become an outmoded and dangerous dream.

Now let me just mention — because this seems to be the heart of the difficulty — what such a concept would *not* mean. It would not imply, first of all, that military strength would not continue to be cultivated on our side until we have better alternatives. The Soviet radio claims that to recognize, as I have done in these talks, that Russia is not yearning to launch an attack on Western Europe means, and I quote their words: "To give up the whole of NATO, the United States bases, and the enormous military expenditure"; in short, the entire Western military structure. What utter nonsense! As though we did not know that any sudden and unilateral Western disarmament would create new political situations and new invitations to aggression where none existed before. Armaments are important not just for what could be done with them in time of war, but for the psychological shadows they cast in time of peace. No one here has forgotten, I trust, the basic hostility borne us by world Communism, the never-ending abuse of our institutions, the shameless distortion of our realities before world opinion, the cynical principles of political struggle, and the sharp, ruthless political tactics that have marked the Russian Communist movement since the moment of its inception. We know what we are up against. Let no one suppose that a recognition of the horrors of nuclear war is going to lead logically to a political and military capitulation on the Western side, any more than it will on the other.

What flows from what I have said is not that one should give up unilaterally the nuclear deterrent, or even that one should desist from the effort to strengthen the NATO forces in Europe. What flows from what I have said is only that war must not be taken as inevitable; that one must not be carried away by the search for absolute security; that certain risks must be assumed in order that greater ones may be avoided; and that NATO must not be strengthened in such a way as to prejudice the chances for an eventual reduction, by peaceful negotiation, of the danger of an all-out war.

Under the concept I have outlined, the military dispositions of NATO would not be an end in themselves but only the means to an end. And this end would not be the achievement of any total solution in the sense of a sudden removal of the political rivalry between the Communist system and our own. It would be the piecemeal removal, by negotiation and compromise, of the major sources of the military danger, particularly the abnormal situation now prevailing in Central and Eastern Europe, and the gradual achievement of a state of affairs in which the political competition could take its course without the constant threat of a general war. There is no use looking any

further than this. Our first concern must be to achieve what is, or might be, immediately possible. After that, we shall see.

And not only can the strengthening of NATO *not* be a substitute for negotiation, but NATO cannot itself provide either the source of authority or the channel for the negotiating process. The governmental structures of the individual NATO members are already of such ponderous and frightening complexity in themselves that it sometimes seems to me questionable whether they would be capable of providing the imagination, the privacy of deliberation, the speed of decision, and the constancy of style necessary to the pursuit of any delicate diplomatic undertaking, even if they were not encumbered with their obligations to allies. What will the situation be if we multiply the ponderousness by a factor of fifteen? A negotiating position into which there is assiduously inserted every last inhibition of every one of fifteen governments will never be a position sufficiently bold and generous to serve as a proper basis for composing issues as complex and stubborn as those that must now be cleared away between Russia and the West. This talk will have to be tackled first by individual governments, within the limits of their competence and with reference to those objects of controversy which lie within their control. The main outlines of settlement will then have to find, at the proper time and in the proper way, the understanding and acquiescence of those whose responsibilities are less directly involved.

It is also idle to suppose that the strengthening of NATO could alone provide the necessary climate and background for negotiation. It cannot be too often reiterated that our contest with Soviet power is of so pervasive and subtle a nature that our purpose cannot be served by any single agency of policy, such as the military one. It is the sum total of our performance that counts; our effort must embrace all facets of our national behavior. Moscow fights with all the political and psychological means at its command; and it will know how to take advantage, as indeed it already has in many ways, of any one-sided concentration of effort on our part. This is why we cannot afford to put all our eggs in the military basket and neglect the positive purposes — the things which we ought to be doing, and would be doing, if the military threat were not upon us at all. The fortunes of the cold war will begin to turn in our direction as and when we learn to apply ourselves resolutely to many things that have, superficially viewed, nothing whatsoever to do with the cold war at all.

Let us, then, while keeping our guard up and while never ceasing to explore the possibilities for progress by negotiation, not neglect those undertakings that are necessary for the spiritual and economic advancement of Western society. There is so much to be done. Our friends on the Continent have recently made exciting progress, despite all military danger, in welding the economic and technological efforts of the Western European peoples into a single competitive yet collaborative whole, and in moderating the sharp edges of that absolute sovereignty which is one of the anachronisms of our time. All power to them; and all admiration for having had the steadfastness to get on with these things at the time when the sputnik was whirling overhead. Surely there is room for something of the same courage and vision in the ordering of the relationships between England, Canada and the United States: for the overcoming of the pound-dollar division and the establishment of common policies in those areas where our concerns and responsibilities

are common. This, too, was envisaged in the original Marshall Plan concept; but it was one of the things that got lost somewhere in the military shuffle. Can it not today be recovered? There is nothing in all this that need worry our continental allies. It changes nothing in our military commitments and arrangements. Is it not perfectly clear that NATO will never be stronger than the degree of intimacy and collaboration that prevails within its English-speaking component?

This is only an example of the things that await doing on the international level, but beyond this there is the whole great area of domestic affairs. Let us not forget this, precisely in the present connection. Many of us dislike to think of domestic problems as battlefields on which, again, our contest with Soviet power is transpiring; but that is exactly what they are. In a thousand ways, the tone and spirit that characterize our internal life impinge themselves on our external fortunes.

Our diplomacy can never be stronger than the impression we contrive to create on others, not just by virtue of what we *do* but rather — and even more importantly — by what we *are*. What greater error could there conceivably be than the belief that weapons, however terrible, could ever protect selfishness, timidity, shortsightedness and lassitude from the penalty that awaits them, over the long run, in the general competition of international life? What greater error than to suppose that such things as courage and vigor and confidence cannot assert themselves in world affairs without the aid of the hydrogen bomb?

Russia confronts us not just with a foreign policy or a military policy but with an integrated philosophy of action, internal and external. We can respond effectively in no other way.

Let us not look, therefore, to the council tables of NATO to provide the basic strength on which the security of the Western world must rest. The statesmen there can work only with what they have. Of this, the armies and weapons are only the smaller part. The greater part lies still in what we of this generation are — first of all to ourselves, secondarily to others. If it is really a new wind that needs to blow through our lives, to enable us to meet successfully the scorn and hostility brought to us by world Communism, then let us open our windows to it and let us brace ourselves to the buffeting we must expect.

In the conclusion of the X-article, to which I referred at the outset of these talks, I cited a passage from the American writer Thoreau. Today, under the shadow of the hydrogen bomb and of all the materialism and faintheartedness of our time, I am going to recall this passage to mind once more. It is, unfortunately, even more relevant today than it was ten years ago.

"There is no ill," Thoreau wrote, "which may not be dissipated, like the dark, if you let in a stronger light upon it. . . . If the light we use is but a paltry and narrow taper, most objects will cast a shadow wider than themselves."

Dean Acheson: THE ILLUSION OF DISENGAGEMENT

Dean Acheson, former Secretary of State under Truman and an architect of NATO, denounced Kennan's plea for disengagement as an incitement to the Soviet Union. Europe was still in danger in 1958; Soviet power in many respects was more awesome than in the past, and any relaxation of vigilance could tempt the Russians to new adventures in Europe. If such a policy were implemented it would "abandon the efforts of a decade, which are bringing closer to realization the hopes of Western Europe, of Germany, and of Eastern Europe as well."

SINCE the war, therefore, the foreign policy of the United States has become, by necessity, a positive and activist one. It has been one of attempting to draw together, through various groupings, that Western area which must be the center of a free and open world system, and of taking the leading part in providing it with military security, and with a developing economy in which trade could grow and industrial productivity could be developed, both in areas which were already industrially advanced and those which were at the threshold.

At the same time it was an essential part of this policy to produce the maximum degree of cohesion throughout the whole non-Communist area, through political policies which would make for integration and strength rather than for exploitation.

Various aspects of this effort — the military, the economic, the political — I have attempted to describe in some detail elsewhere. I have there pointed out the interdependence of the Western Hemisphere and Western Europe; how the power factors involved make it essen-

Excerpted by special permission from *Foreign Affairs*, XXXVI (April, 1958), pp. 373–381. Copyright by the Council on Foreign Relations, Inc., New York.

tial that this part of the world shall stand firmly united; how, without the American connection, it is impossible to maintain independent national life in Western Europe; and how, without Western Europe, the power factors would turn disastrously against the United States.

Broadly speaking, these conceptions have for the past decade or more had wide acceptance both in this country and throughout the Western world. They have been successful beyond the dream of those who first advocated them. They are beginning to bear the most valuable fruit.

Recently, efforts have been relaxed. Our military security and much of our prestige resting upon it have been impaired, though not so far that vigorous action cannot make the necessary repair. But, throughout the world, as I indicated at the beginning of this article, voices are being raised to ask whether it is necessary to continue facing the hazards of the military situation, to continue bearing the expense of making vital and progressive the economic life of the whole free world; whether coexistence with the Communist system cannot be bought at a cheaper price and with less effort. And so, when people are told, as they have been by Mr. George Kennan, a man of the highest character and reputation and justly entitled to a respectful hearing, that this is possible, his words have a powerful impact.

Mr. Kennan's views are not new to him. They do not spring from a fresh analysis of the current situation. He has held and expressed these views for at least a decade. The effect which they have had currently makes us realize anew that the reception given to the expression of ideas depends upon the mood of the hearers. This reception may have little to do with the truth of the ideas expressed; it has a great deal to do with

their power. Mr. Kennan has told people what they want to hear, though not because they want to hear it. What is it that he has said?

The ideas are almost as vague as the style is seductive. The thoughts are expressed as musings, wonderings, questionings, suggestions. But what comes out of it is about this: First, there is the idea of disengagement in Europe. By this is meant mutual withdrawal of American, British and Canadian, as well as Russian, forces from somewhere. This somewhere first appears to be East and West Germany; then the "heart of Europe;" again, the Continent; and sometimes, from the general ethos of the discussion, it appears to be all overseas areas.

The second idea is the neutralization of Germany. The third is that there should be no nuclear weapons in Europe. And the fourth is that throughout Asia and Africa, in what are called the "uncommitted areas," there is little "to be done . . . except to relax;" that "It is perfectly natural that Russia . . . should have her place and her voice there too;" that "our generation in the West" has no "obligation vis-à-vis the underdeveloped parts of the world," and, anyway, there is no "absolute value attached to rapid economic development. Why all the urgency?" If any sound schemes for development are presented, we should support them, "when they arise;" but, only on the condition that they tell us first "how you propose to assure that if we give you this aid it will not be interpreted among your people as a sign of weakness and fear on our part, or of a desire to dominate you." If Asian and African states should find in this grudging, meager and humiliating policy no opportunity to push their economic development within the non-Communist system, and should turn to Communist methods and Communist help, we should accept their action without concern and with good nature.

One sees at once that these conceptions are the very opposite of those which the West has been following for the past ten years or more. It is an assertion that the struggle naught availeth; that it is dangerous, unwise and unproductive. It is a withdrawal from positive and active leadership in the creation of a workable system of states. It is a conception, blended of monasticism and the diplomacy of earlier centuries, by which the United States would artfully manoeuvre its way between and around forces without attempting to direct or control them.

If we attempt to analyze these suggestions, the problems which they create promptly emerge. First, let us consider the idea that something called disengagement can be brought about by removing American, British, Canadian and Russian troops from some area in Europe. What disengagement does this bring about? Very little, as one sees if one pauses to consider the realities. Compare the confrontation which takes place between the United States and the Soviet Union in Germany with that which occurs along the DEW line — that system of early warning stations which stretches from Alaska, across the Arctic regions and far out into the Atlantic. Here there are daily contacts on a thousand radarscopes, and doubtless the same is true on the other side of the screen. Some of these blips on the radar are actual aircraft; sometimes atmospheric conditions produce them. But they represent a contact which no action in Germany can disengage. There is confrontation in every part of the world where the area of the open and free world system may be reduced by Soviet military, economic or political penetration. No action in Ger-

many will produce disengagement here. The word is a mere conception, which confuses and does not represent any reality.

So, let us turn from it to consider something more capable of delineation. For instance, exactly what is the extent of the mutual withdrawal about which we are asked to negotiate? The answer to this question does not depend upon penetrating the vagueness of Mr. Kennan's language. For there can be little doubt, I believe, that, once a withdrawal begins, it will be complete, so far as United States, British and Canadian troops are concerned. All the forces, foreign and domestic, will combine to bring this about. As the withdrawal makes the military position weaker, our forces will be less desired wherever they may remain. If withdrawal is represented as advantageous for Germans, it would seem equally advantageous to Frenchmen. Icelanders, Moroccans, Saudi Arabians and the rest would quickly follow. And, once the idea caught hold, Americans would, of course, join in the general demand. The *New Statesman* shows us how the matter is now being presented to a small section of British opinion and how it could bemuse a still larger one in that country:

Yet the missile agreement is one of the most extraordinary and complete surrenders of sovereignty ever to be made by one country for the exclusive benefit of another. For the missiles are not intended to defend Britain; on the contrary, they decisively increase its vulnerability. Their prime purpose is to reduce the likelihood of a Soviet ICBM onslaught on America during the crucial three-year period which must elapse before America possesses ICBMs herself. The sole beneficiary will be America.

We should not deceive ourselves. After disengagement, we would soon find ourselves discussing complete withdrawal from all European areas and, very possibly, from bases in the Far East and Near East as well. Indeed, Mr. Khrushchev has twice served warning, once in Berlin in 1957 and again in January of 1958, that the sort of withdrawal which he is talking about is withdrawal from all overseas bases. This would cut the striking power of the free world by at least a half, and, perhaps, until our missile program accelerates, by much more.

We must think of what we purchase for this vast price. What would Russian withdrawal from Germany or the heart of Europe amount to? Is it possible to believe that the Soviet Government, whatever it may say or whatever agreement it may sign, would, or could, contemplate withdrawing its forces behind, say, the River Bug, and keeping them there? And, by forces, I mean effective Russian physical power, by whatever name called. It is hard to see, after the events in Poland and Hungary, whatever the Russian Government might wish, how it could possibly undertake so hazardous a course. For, if its physical force were permanently removed from Eastern Europe, who can believe that even one of the Communist régimes would survive? Therefore, wherever Soviet forces might be garrisoned, the expectation and threat of their return must continue to be ever present (at most it would require from 12 to 18 hours) if Russia is to maintain the power which it has insisted upon as recently as the Hungarian uprising.

At this point in our discussion we must examine the conception of the neutralization of Germany; and then bring together the consequences of withdrawal and neutralization. It is necessary, we are told, that Germany should not be allowed to be free to choose its own course after unification. It must accept limitations upon its military forces and its military alignment. In other words, its national life will be conducted under far greater limitations than those in which other sovereign people live. The possibility that any such situation could endure seems to me quite fantastic.

Whatever Germans might initially think they would be willing to do, there is no precedent in history for, nor does there seem to me to be any possibility of, the successful insulation of a large and vital country situated, as Germany is, between two power systems and with ambitions and purposes of its own. Constant strain would undermine the sanctions of neutralization. The final result would be determined by the relative strength of the pressures from the two sides. As I have already suggested, the pressure would all be from the Russian side. For, there would be no Power in Europe capable of opposing Russian will after the departure of the United States from the Continent and the acceptance of a broad missile-free area. Then, it would not be long, I fear, before there would be an accommodation of some sort or another between an abandoned Germany and the great Power to the East. Under this accommodation, a sort of new Ribbentrop-Molotov agreement, the rest of the free world would be faced with what has twice been so intolerable as to provoke world war — the unification of the European land mass (this time the Eurasian land mass) under a Power hostile to national independence and individual freedom.

But, without this withdrawal of forces and the neutralization of Germany, Mr. Kennan sees "little hope for any removal of the division of Germany at all — nor, by the same token, of the removal of the division of Europe." Naturally enough, these words have found a strong echo in Germany. But it is a fading one, as Germans ponder the conditions which would flow from unification by withdrawal and neutralization, and see the end of the best hopes of the German people. Two weak states — East and West Germany — jockeying for position in a sort of no-man's land, could raise the East-West "tensions" to a point compared to which anything we have yet experienced would seem mild indeed. In all this West Berlin would, of course, be the first victim. It would be a wholly inadequate judgment upon those whose naïveté and weakness produced this result that they should share the guilt of those Western politicians whose preaching of "liberation" encouraged the uprisings in East Berlin and Hungary, and, like them, should sit in supine impotence while more gallant men suffered. The best hope for German unification I shall mention shortly.

Turning to Eastern Europe, Mr. Kennan sees those countries, without the withdrawal of Russian troops, caught between the dilemma of constant revolutions, bloodily suppressed, and the acknowledgment of Soviet domination. This view seems to me founded on nothing but its assertion. I cannot for the life of me see how the movement toward a greater degree of national identity in Eastern Europe is furthered by removing from the Continent the only Power capable of opposing the Soviet Union.

Nor do I see that the facts bear out Mr. Kennan's gloomy predictions. For instance, if the experience of 1956 had produced only the development in Poland or if the Hungarians had acted with as much restraint, it would have been plain to all that the attraction of the power of the West, of the possibilities which its system opens to all, was proving very strong indeed — stronger even

than the secret police and Soviet occupation troops. The fact that in Hungary the reaction was pushed to the point where the Russians felt it necessary to suppress it with force proves only that it was handled unwisely.

So, as we think about the matter, we must wonder whether there is anything we can purchase "one-half so precious as the goods" we sell. We are told not to worry about this; that, even though it seems quite unlikely that the Russians would carry out any withdrawal, nevertheless, it is good propaganda to make the offer and cause them to refuse it. This seems to me profoundly false. In the first place, it treats international negotiations as though all the figures on the chessboard were made of wood or ivory; whereas, in fact, we are dealing with living people, subject to all the emotions of mankind. If I were a European and had to live through two or three years of American negotiations about withdrawing from the Continent, I think that very early in the game I would discount America's remaining and would prepare to face a new situation. Furthermore, to believe that the Russians can be put in the position of refusing to evacuate Europe underrates their skill in negotiation. They would simply, as they have already done, continue to raise the price. And it would be we and not they who would do the refusing.

The evils of a timid and defeatist policy of retreat are far deeper than its ineptness as a move in the propaganda battle. It would abandon the efforts of a decade, which are bringing closer to realization the hopes of Western Europe, of Germany, and of Eastern Europe as well. From the low point of 1946–1947 the economic, social and political health and strength of Western Europe — of which West Germany has become an integral and vital part — have grown greatly. Their pull on Eastern Europe continues to mount. To continue this the American connection is essential. The success of the movement toward unity in the west of Europe is no longer in doubt. Only the rate of progress is undecided. The Coal and Steel Community, Euratom, the Common Market have been accepted. A common currency and political community are on the way.

All of this is threatened by the call to retreat. It will not do to say that a united Germany, made militarily impotent and neutralized, can play an effective part in bringing to fruition a united and vigorous European community. The slightest puff of reality blows this wishful fancy away. The jockeyings and tensions of the two parts of Germany, the unopposable threat of Russian power, the bribes which can be dangled before Germany by the Soviet Union in the form of boundary rectifications and economic opportunities — these alone are enough to put an end to hope of a united and strong Europe, invigorated by Germany.

For those who believe that Eastern Europe would welcome American and Russian troop withdrawals as the beginning of liberation, I suggest a quiet sampling of candid Polish opinion. I venture to predict that what they would find is a horror at being abandoned by the West and left between the Soviet Union and a Germany similarly abandoned, to which the offer of another partition of Poland might be irresistible.

But, if one looks at the other side of the medal, what a different face it bears! A strong, united Europe could have the men and the resources — along with British and United States contingents — to deal by conventional forces with invasion by conventional forces, particularly as the Eastern European satellites are be-

coming a danger, and not an asset, to Soviet military power. This, if pressed, gives real mutuality of benefit to a negotiated reduction in forces. It makes possible, too, a time when nuclear forces would no longer have to be relied on as a substitute for conventional forces, and with it a real opportunity to negotiate this threat further and further into the background.

Finally, a thriving Western Europe would continue its irresistible pull upon East Germany and Eastern Europe. This would, in turn, have its effect upon the demands of the Russian people on their government. With a rise in the standards of living in the Soviet Union, and as some broader participation in the direction of affairs was made essential by their very magnitude and complexity, the Russian need for the forced communization and iron control of Eastern Europe would diminish. Then negotiations looking toward a united Germany, under honorable and healing conditions, and toward the return of real national identity to the countries of Eastern Europe, while preserving also the interests of the Russian people in their own security and welfare, could for the first time be meaningful and show the buds of hope. This has been the goal of Western policy for the past decade.

It would be self-delusion to close our eyes to the difficulties which lie before us along this road. Some we have created ourselves. Our military strategy, with its sole reliance on massive retaliation, and a budgetary policy which has neglected even that, have caused us a loss of relative military power and of prestige. Some of our political policies have weakened our alliances. Our allies, too, are having their troubles. In what are perhaps the two closest of them, we could wish (as they undoubtedly do,

too) that both the present and the immediate future held greater promise for the
development of strength and popular
attitudes more attuned to reality. We all
share together the common problem of
devising a military policy for NATO
which will avoid making the proposed
defense seem as fearsome as the potential enemy's threat, and which will be a
real deterrent because it is a credible
one.

I have suggested elsewhere that this is
possible. Briefly, the way is to create a
situation in fact which equals the political purpose of the North Atlantic Treaty
— that is, a situation where in order for
the Soviet Union to attack, or coerce,
Europe it would have to attack, or coerce, the United States as well. This, if
we all use a fair degree of intelligence
about our defenses, the Soviet Union
could be deterred from doing. What is

required is a short-range effort which
does not preclude a sustained effort toward a wiser long-range goal. The short-
range effort would be to provide NATO
with such effective nuclear power that
the Soviet Union could not have its way
without destroying that power; and an
attempt to destroy it would be impracti-
cal apart from a simultaneous attempt to
disable the United States, which could
be made too dangerous. The longer-
range purpose would be to develop adequate conventional forces in Europe,
with British and American participation,
to make mutually desirable a real reduction and equalization of both Soviet and
NATO forces and a controlled elimination of nuclear material for military use.

I quite understand that all of this is
difficult. But I believe also that "the
mode by which the inevitable comes to
pass is effort."

Henry Kissinger: AMERICAN STRATEGY AND NATO — A TEST CASE

*Henry A. Kissinger, Professor of Government at Harvard and direc-
tor of Harvard's Defense Studies Program, wrote an influential book in
1958 which found a middle path for NATO between Kennan's disengagement and Acheson's recommendations for a massive nuclear
weaponry. He urged that advantage be taken of increasingly sophisticated nuclear warfare in which tactical nuclear weapons would become
the basis for an adequate strategy of local defense by European members of NATO.*

FROM a military point of view, NATO's
difficulties are due to its inability to
resolve two issues in terms which are
meaningful to all partners: the purpose
of a military establishment on the Continent, and the implications of nuclear

weapons for allied strategy. So long as
the United States and Britain base their
strategy on the assumption that any war
in Europe will inevitably lead to all-out
war and that all-out war will necessarily
be fought as an intercontinental ther-

From Henry A. Kissinger, *Nuclear Weapons and Foreign Policy*, pp. 306–315. Published by Harper
& Brothers for the Council on Foreign Affairs and reprinted by permission of the Council on Foreign
Relations, Inc.

monuclear exchange, there is an inherent imbalance between their interest in the alliance and that of the other NATO powers. No soothing statements can bridge the gulf between our allies' concern with local defense and the requirements of an all-out strategy. The very location of our air bases along the periphery of Eurasia and beyond, in Spain, Morocco and Saudi Arabia, testifies to the dispensability of the Continental powers. This imbalance has caused NATO's military strategy to be built on a series of compromises, on concessions by us to European fears and reluctant concessions by the European members to our insistence on a military contribution by them. The result has been a proliferation of military establishments on the Continent, too strong to serve as a trip-wire, too weak to resist a Soviet onslaught, and in any case, not really designed for that purpose. NATO has evolved in a never-never land, where our strategic doctrine has undermined the European incentive to make a substantial military effort, while the Europeans have been reluctant to make their hesitations explicit lest we withdraw the guarantee of their frontiers which, in terms of an all-out strategy, has been NATO's only really meaningful function.

Nothing is more important, therefore, than to be clear about the role we wish NATO to perform. Is it a device to serve warning on the Soviet bloc that an attack on Western Europe will inevitably unleash an all-out war? Or is it designed to assure the integrity of Europe against attack? In the former case there is little point in maintaining large British, American and Canadian forces on the Continent, and the European military buildup in turn is bound to be ambivalent, hesitant and essentially meaningless. In the latter case, a radical adjustment is

required in our strategic doctrine and in supporting policies.

Ever since the end of World War II, one notion has been repeated so often that it has virtually acquired the status of a dogma: that only the atom bomb and our retaliatory power stand between the Red Army and the occupation of Europe, and that any attack on Europe must inevitably unleash all-out war. On behalf of this proposition several reasons are advanced: Europe is a "vital" interest and, therefore, must receive the protection of our massive deterrent, whereas local wars are appropriate only for objectives of peripheral importance. Strategic air war is our only possible riposte to a Soviet attack on Europe, because we cannot afford to match Soviet manpower or engage the Red Army in a war of attrition. We have no choice, so the argument usually concludes, but to fight an all-out war because our NATO partners will look askance at any defense of their territories which involves the local use of nuclear weapons.

The most unchallenged arguments often inhibit clear thought most severely. It is a strange doctrine which asserts that vital interests can be defended only by the most catastrophic strategy. To be sure, we must be prepared to defend our vital interests by all-out war, if necessary. But this is a far cry from asserting that we must *begin* that defense with a thermonuclear holocaust or that it is not to our interest to develop alternative strategies. Less cataclysmic strategic options are all the more important because of the very reason formerly advanced for an all-out strategy: that it would prevent a long drawn-out contest of attrition. Given the power of modern weapons, all-out war now makes inevitable the very result which our reliance on an all-out strategy immediately after World

War II sought to prevent: whatever the outcome of an all-out war, it will drain, perhaps destroy, the national substance. And if during a thermonuclear exchange the Red Army takes over Europe, we will not have sufficient resources left to liberate our allies. All-out war may forestall neither attrition nor Soviet occupation of Europe.

Nor is the argument based on our inadequate manpower conclusive. The combined manpower of the United States and its European allies has always exceeded that of the Soviet bloc in Europe. The disparity has not been the availability of manpower, but the willingness to mobilize it. Moreover, the advent of tactical nuclear weapons in quantity makes the difference in mobilized manpower strategically less significant, provided we and our allies are prepared to draw the consequences from the strategic revolution that has occurred and are willing to face up to the problem of limited nuclear war. On a nuclear battlefield there is an inherent upper limit to the number of troops that can be strategically significant. While this number is larger than the present NATO force, it is not so large as to be beyond the realm of possibility. It presupposes, however, a diplomacy which establishes a clear understanding of the nature of limited nuclear war on the part of our allies and, perhaps more importantly, by our opponent.

Will not a limited nuclear war in Europe cause such widespread devastation as to defeat its purpose? Is not the lesson of "Carte Blanche" that a limited nuclear war would mean the end of European civilization just as surely as an all-out war? An all-out strategy is advocated by many in the belief that a limited nuclear war would reduce the battle zone to "radioactive rubble" and that this pros-

pect will inhibit our allies' will to resist. It is contradictory, however, to argue that our allies will be reluctant to undertake a limited war in defense of their territories but that we will remain prepared to implement an all-out strategy which would be infinitely more destructive. Why should Britain and the United States be ready to accept complete devastation when the countries most directly concerned shrink from much less drastic measures? Nor is it clear what reassurance allies which are to be saved from being turned into radioactive rubble can derive from the fact that in the consequence of an all-out war we share their fate.

Moreover, the argument in favor of a strategy of limited nuclear war is that it would keep the world from being turned into radioactive rubble. As we have seen, a limited nuclear war would approach all-out war in destructiveness only if it should be conducted with the tactics of World War II, with fixed lines, massive attacks on communication centers and an attempt to wipe out the enemy industrial potential. The lessons of "Carte Blanche" are therefore deceptive. In the near future — as strategic doctrine goes, within ten years — the massive attack on opposing air installations will become strategically unproductive or unnecessary. With the advent of missiles and vertical take-off aircraft there will be no need to drop some three hundred atomic devices within forty-eight hours. The key goal in a limited nuclear war should not be to eliminate enemy communication centers but to prevent an enemy from controlling territory by keeping him from concentrating large bodies of troops in the contested area. A limited nuclear war should not be compared to a ground war in the traditional sense. Its units ideally should approximate the mobility of an air force but they should be capable of forcing the enemy either to concentrate his forces and thus to present a target, or so to disperse his forces that he will not be able to impose his political domination.

Other proponents of an all-out strategy have argued that an attempt to undertake local defense would serve Soviet interests because it would deliver the great prize of Western Europe into its hands undestroyed. "If we say that atomic weapons may be used only in the area of the front line . . . ," writes Sir John Slessor,

it will not ring a very cordial bell with our new NATO allies, and Russia herself would be immune except possibly for towns in the immediate neighbourhood of airfields. That seems to be a good bargain for the Russians who would surely rather capture places like Paris and the Channel ports intact than as masses of radio-active rubble.

It is contradictory to maintain that it may be to our interest to bring about a widespread devastation of the areas we seek to protect by a deliberately chosen strategy. It is not apparent why the adoption by the West of a strategy of massive retaliation would force the U.S.S.R. into destroying Paris or the Channel ports. On the contrary, in an all-out war the important targets would seem to be the United States and perhaps the British strategic air bases. This does not mean that a strategy of all-out war would be to the advantage of our European allies. Even if our allies should escape the direct effect of bombing, the problems of fall-out, of strontium-90, and of genetic effects would remain. The danger that unrestricted thermonuclear war might make life unsupportable and the fear of the ravages of Soviet occupa-

tion should be a powerful incentive for them to undertake local defense.

A strategy looking to the local defense of Europe should not be considered as a device for holding our alliance together. On the contrary, the alliance should be conceived as a means to bring about the common defense by means which do not involve national catastrophe for all partners. Such a strategy is impossible, however, until our allies have a better understanding of the nature of nuclear technology and, therefore, of the nature of limited nuclear war. One of the banes of our alliance policy has been the exclusion of the Continental powers from the nuclear race, in part because of the restrictions imposed on the exchange of information by the United States Atomic Energy Act. But it will not prove possible in the long run to maintain a strategy whose chief weapon is in the exclusive control of the two allies geographically most remote from the first line of Soviet advance. Since our allies possess neither a substantial nuclear technology, nor an arsenal of nuclear weapons, they are assailed by a sense of impotence and can fall easy prey to Soviet propaganda, which seeks to picture nuclear weapons as a category of special horror. If the United States retains exclusive control of nuclear weapons our allies will become increasingly vulnerable to Soviet atomic blackmail, which implies that they can escape their dilemmas by refusing to adopt a nuclear strategy. The success of this tactic in an area outside NATO is illustrated by the announcement of the Japanese Government that none of the United States atomic support commands would be permitted to be stationed on Japanese soil.

One of the chief tasks of United States policy in NATO, therefore, is to overcome the trauma which attaches to the use of nuclear weapons and to decentralize the possession of nuclear weapons as rapidly as possible. Nothing would so much dispel the air of mystery that surrounds nuclear weapons as their possession by the Continental powers. Nothing would do more to help restore a measure of consistency to allied military planning. The rationale for the secrecy imposed by the Atomic Energy Act has long since disappeared. It made sense only so long as we possessed an atomic monopoly. But with the growth of the Soviet nuclear stockpile, our allies have become the real victims of our policy of withholding atomic information. They are either forced into a wasteful duplication of effort and into research long since accomplished by the United States and the U.S.S.R. or else they are obliged to rely on military establishments hopelessly at a disadvantage vis-à-vis that of the Soviet Union.

Almost as important as the possession of nuclear weapons would be the acquisition by our NATO partners of missiles, at least of intermediary range. Since most of European Russia is vulnerable to missiles with a range of 1,500 miles, the existence of this capability would place Europe in a better position to withstand the threat of a Soviet rocket attack, a threat which proved so effective during the Suez crisis. The agreement between President Eisenhower and Prime Minister Harold Macmillan to make United States missiles available to Britain is a hopeful step in a direction which could become a model for all of NATO.

The possession of nuclear weapons and missiles will not by itself solve NATO's difficulties, however. On the contrary, it may become one more argument for a reduction of forces and one more temptation to stake everything on an all-out retaliatory strategy. And a strategy of massive retaliation may cause the alliance to recoil before resisting any except the most dire and unambiguous challenges. In order to escape the paralysis induced by such prospects NATO must adopt a doctrine which shows the relevance of the new weapons to a strategy less catastrophic than all-out war.

The leadership in this effort must be taken by the United States. Only the United States possesses the technical know-how which can give meaning to a European defense contribution. Only the United States possesses the retaliatory force which can furnish the shield for a local defense. Unless the United States, in its doctrine and its military establishment, demonstrates its faith in the local defense of Europe, the military effort of NATO will lack a sense of direction. There is no point in adding conventional German divisions to an Anglo-American army equipped with nuclear weapons and backed by a tactical air force which is based almost exclusively on a nuclear strategy. A logistics system of World War II vintage based on a few supply centers, each completely vulnerable to nuclear attack, is highly dangerous if our strategy envisages the possibility of using nuclear weapons. NATO's present cumbersome structure is hardly suitable for the rapid reaction required by nuclear war. The conventional armies of our Continental allies may actually prove an impediment on a nuclear battlefield. NATO will, therefore, have to be adapted to the nuclear period both doctrinally and organizationally. The armies of our allies, or at least that part of them earmarked for Europe, should be equipped and trained for nuclear war. And the alliance should strive to gain acceptance for a strategic doctrine which does not identify nuclear war with all-out war. NATO, in short, must seek to escape its present inconsistencies. It is either a device to defend Europe locally or an instrument to unleash the British and American strategic air forces. It cannot be both and it cannot be the former without a more realistic defense effort by our European allies.

Should our allies prove reluctant to support even a militarily revitalized NATO, it would seem time to put an end to the half-measures that have hamstrung the military effort of the alliance. In the absence of a more substantial European defense effort, five American and four British divisions are too little to assure local defense and too much for internal security purposes. The presence of less than half that number would amply demonstrate our determination and insure our participation in an all-out war. In the absence of a military structure capable of achieving local defense, the protection of Europe resides essentially in the willingness of the United States and Great Britain to undertake all-out war in response to Soviet aggression. This determination could be conveyed with less ambiguity through a reduction of United States and British strength in Europe, for it would remove any assumption that an attack on Europe would be dealt with by local defense.

The North Atlantic Treaty Organization has thus come to a fork in the road. It can no longer reconcile an all-out strategy with an inadequate and half-hearted effort of local defense. It must decide soon whether NATO represents a variation on the Monroe Doctrine — defining a region which will be protected essentially by a unilateral United States guarantee — or whether it can be made to serve what has become the most productive and least costly strategy: the strategy of a local defense based on nuclear weapons.

Our European allies must realize that in the nuclear age they do not have the resources to maintain a military establishment for both limited and all-out war. Any effort to do so will reduce the overall effectiveness without adding to their individual strength. Their most meaningful contribution is in the capability for limited war. As for us, while we should do everything we can to assure an adequate basis for the defense of Europe, anything short of an establishment capable of local defense will result in a dispersal of resources.

Much has been made of strengthening the nonmilitary side of NATO, but such proposals will remain palliatives until NATO faces up to the military facts. A defensive alliance cannot be maintained unless it develops some notion of the nature of common defense.

The willingness to undertake a local defense of Europe will be a test whether the alliance can be adapted to conditions radically changed from those that were foreseen at its initiation. The effort to call the North Atlantic Treaty Organization into being has been so considerable, that we may be tempted to overlook the fact that a strategy developed when we enjoyed an atomic monopoly is no longer adequate to a period of nuclear plenty. The free world, which has been challenged to protect its political beliefs, is also asked to demonstrate the resilience of its strategic thinking. If NATO cannot develop a strategy less catastrophic than all-out war, its determination cannot be expected to survive the perils which will inevitably confront it. It may be that neither we nor our European allies will be prepared to make the economic sacrifices required for such a course. But at least we should not confuse in our own minds the least burdensome with the most effective strategy. The result of an attempt to

evade the strategic problem may be catastrophe in case of war and a steady
deterioration of the cohesiveness of the
alliance during periods of peace.

The shape of future strategy cannot be
determined solely by ourselves or by our
allies, however. Rather, our measures
will be relevant only to the extent that
they prove adequate to deal with the
threat which makes the free world's concern with strategy so important in the
first place: the revolutionary challenge of
the Soviet Union and Communist China.

VI. THE FUTURE OF NATO

John F. Kennedy: THE ATLANTIC COMMUNITY

*President Kennedy spoke many times of the broader significance of
the United States' membership in an Atlantic Community. Nowhere
was he more eloquent on this subject than in his tour of Germany in
the summer of 1963. NATO in his vision was a means to the creation
of "a new social order," in which greater reliance should be placed
upon political and economic purposes.*

Dr. Gerstenmaier, President Kiesinger,
Vice Chancellor Erhard, Minister-President Zinn, Mayor Bockelmann, ladies
and gentlemen:

I am most honored, Mr. President, to
be able to speak in this city before this
audience, for in this hall I am able to
address myself to those who lead and
serve all segments of a democratic system — mayors, governors, members of
cabinets, civil servants, and concerned
citizens. As one who has known the satisfaction of the legislator's life, I am particularly pleased that so many members
of your Bundestag and Bundesrat are
present today, for the vitality of your
legislature has been a major factor in
your demonstration of a working democracy, a democracy worldwide in its influence. In your company also are several
of the authors of the Federal Constitution who have been able through their
own political service to give a new and
lasting validity to the aims of the Frankfurt Assembly.

One hundred and fifteen years ago a
most learned Parliament was convened
in this historic hall. Its goal was a united
German Federation. Its members were
poets and professors, lawyers and philosophers, doctors and clergymen, freely

elected in all parts of the land. No nation applauded its endeavors as warmly
as my own. No assembly ever strove
more ardently to put perfection into practice. And though in the end it failed, no
other building in Germany deserves more
the title of "cradle of German democracy."

But can there be such a title? In my
own home city of Boston, Faneuil Hall —
once the meeting-place of the authors of
the American Revolution — has long been
known as the "cradle of American liberty." But when, in 1852, the Hungarian
patriot Kossuth addressed an audience
there, he criticized its name. "It is," he
said,

a great name — but there is something in it
which saddens my heart. You should not
say "American liberty." You should say
"liberty in America." Liberty should not be
either American or European — it should
just be "liberty."

Kossuth was right. For unless liberty
flourishes in all lands, it cannot flourish
in one. Conceived in one hall, it must
be carried out in many. Thus, the seeds
of the American Revolution had been
brought earlier from Europe, and they
later took root around the world. And

From John F. Kennedy, address in the Assembly Hall at the Paulskirche in Frankfurt, June 25, 1963.
Public Papers of the President (1963), pp. 516–521.

the German Revolution of 1848 transmitted ideas and idealists to America and to other lands. Today, in 1963, democracy and liberty are more international than ever before. And the spirit of the Frankfurt Assembly, like the spirit of Faneuil Hall, must live in many hearts and nations if it is to live at all.

For we live in an age of interdependence as well as independence — an age of internationalism as well as nationalism. In 1848 many countries were indifferent to the goals of the Frankfurt Assembly. It was, they said, a German problem. Today there are no exclusively German problems, or American problems, or even European problems. There are world problems — and our two countries and continents are inextricably bound together in the tasks of peace as well as war.

We are partners for peace — not in a narrow bilateral context but in a framework of Atlantic partnership. The ocean divides us less than the Mediterranean divided the ancient world of Greece and Rome. Our Constitution is old and yours is young, and our culture is young and yours is old, but in our commitment we can and must speak and act with but one voice. Our roles are distinct but complementary — and our goals are the same: peace and freedom for all men, for all time, in a world of abundance, in a world of justice.

That is why our nations are working together to strengthen NATO, to expand trade, to assist the developing countries, to align our monetary policies and to build the Atlantic Community. I would not diminish the miracle of West Germany's economic achievements. But the true German miracle has been your rejection of the past for the future — your reconciliation with France, your participation in the building of Europe, your

leading role in NATO, and your growing support for constructive undertakings throughout the world.

Your economic institutions, your constitutional guarantees, your confidence in civilian authority, are all harmonious with the ideals of older democracies. And they form a firm pillar of the democratic European Community.

But Goethe tells us in his greatest poem that Faust lost the liberty of his soul when he said to the passing moment: "Stay, thou art so fair." And our liberty, too, is endangered if we pause for the passing moment, if we rest on our achievements, if we resist the pace of progress. For time and the world do not stand still. Change is the law of life. And those who look only to the past or the present are certain to miss the future.

The future of the West lies in Atlantic partnership — a system of cooperation, interdependence, and harmony whose peoples can jointly meet their burdens and opportunities throughout the world. Some say this is only a dream, but I do not agree. A generation of achievement — the Marshall plan, NATO, the Schuman plan, and the Common Market — urges us up the path to greater unity.

There will be difficulties and delays. There will be doubts and discouragement. There will be differences of approach and opinion. But we have the will and the means to serve three related goals — the heritage of our countries, the unity of our continents, and the interdependence of the Western alliance.

Some say that the United States will neither hold to these purposes nor abide by its pledges — that we will revert to a narrow nationalism. But such doubts fly in the face of history. For 18 years the United States has stood its watch for freedom all around the globe. The firmness of American will, and the effectiveness of American strength, have been shown, in support of free men and free government, in Asia, in Africa, in the Americas, and, above all, here in Europe. We have undertaken, and sustained in honor, relations of mutual trust and obligation with more than 40 allies. We are proud of this record, which more than answers doubts. But in addition these proven commitments to the common freedom and safety are assured, in the future as in the past, by one great fundamental fact — that they are deeply rooted in America's own self-interest. Our commitment to Europe is indispensable — in our interest as well as yours.

It is not in our interest to try to dominate the European councils of decision. If that were our objective, we would prefer to see Europe divided and weak, enabling the United States to deal with each fragment individually. Instead we have and now look forward to a Europe united and strong — speaking with a common voice — a world power capable of meeting world problems as a full and equal partner.

This is in the interest of us all. For war in Europe, as we learned twice in 40 years, destroys peace in America. A threat to the freedom of Europe is a threat to the freedom of America. That is why no administration — no administration — in Washington can fail to respond to such a threat — not merely from good will but from necessity. And that is why we look forward to a united Europe in an Atlantic partnership — an entity of interdependent parts, sharing equally both burdens and decisions, and linked together in the tasks of defense as well as the arts of peace.

This is no fantasy. It will be achieved by concrete steps to solve the problems that face us all: military, economic, and political. Partnership is not a posture but a process — a continuous process that

grows stronger each year as we devote ourselves to common tasks.

The first task of the Atlantic Community was to assure its common defense. That defense was and still is indivisible. The United States will risk its cities to defend yours because we need your freedom to protect ours. Hundreds of thousands of our soldiers serve with yours on this continent, as tangible evidence of that pledge. Those who would doubt our pledge or deny this indivisibility — those who would separate Europe from America or split one ally from another — would only give aid and comfort to the men who make themselves our adversaries and welcome any Western disarray.

The purpose of our common military effort is not war but peace — not the destruction of nations but the protection of freedom. The forces that West Germany contributes to this effort are second to none among the Western European nations. Your nation is in the front line of defense — and your divisions, side by side with our own, are a source of strength to us all.

These conventional forces are essential, and they are backed by the sanction of thousands of the most modern weapons here on European soil and thousands more, only minutes away, in posts around the world. Together our nations have developed for the forward defense of free Europe a deterrent far surpassing the present or prospective force of any hostile power.

Nevertheless, it is natural that America's nuclear position has raised questions within the alliance. I believe we must confront these questions — not by turning the clock backward to separate nuclear deterrents — but by developing a more closely unified Atlantic deterrent, with genuine European participation. How this can best be done, and it is not easy — in some ways more difficult to split the atom politically than it was physically, but how this can best be done is now under discussion with those who may wish to join in this effort. The proposal before us is for a new Atlantic force. Such a force would bring strength instead of weakness, cohesion instead of division. It would belong to all members, not one, with all participating on a basis of full equality. And as Europe moves towards unity, its role and responsibility, here as elsewhere, would and must increase accordingly.

Meanwhile, there is much to do. We must work more closely together on strategy, training, and planning. European officers from NATO are being assigned to the Strategic Air Command Headquarters in Omaha, Nebr. Modern weapons are being deployed here in Western Europe. And America's strategic deterrent — the most powerful in history — will continue to be at the service of the whole alliance.

Second: Our partnership is not military alone. *Economic* unity is also imperative — not only among the nations of Europe, but across the wide Atlantic.

Indeed, economic cooperation is needed throughout the entire free world. By opening our markets to the developing countries of Africa, Asia, and Latin America, by contributing our capital and our skills, by stabilizing basic prices, we can help assure them of a favorable climate for freedom and growth. This is an Atlantic responsibility. For the Atlantic nations themselves helped to awaken these peoples. Our merchants and our traders ploughed up their soils — and their societies as well — in search of minerals and oil and rubber and coffee. Now we must help them gain full membership in the 20th century, closing the gap between rich and poor.

Another great economic challenge is the coming round of trade negotiations. Those deliberations are much more important than a technical discussion of trade and commerce. They are an opportunity to build common industrial and agricultural policies across the Atlantic. They are an opportunity to open up new sources of demand to give new impetus to growth, and make more jobs and prosperity, for our expanding populations. They are an opportunity to recognize the trading needs and aspirations of other free world countries, including Japan.

In short, these negotiations are a test of our unity. While each nation must naturally look out for its own interests, each nation must also look out for the common interest — the need for greater markets on both sides of the Atlantic — the need to reduce the imbalance between developed and underdeveloped nations — and the need to stimulate the Atlantic economy to higher levels of production rather than to stifle it by higher levels of protection.

We must not return to the 1930's when we exported to each other our own stagnation. We must not return to the discredited view that trade favors some nations at the expense of others. Let no one think that the United States — with only a fraction of its economy dependent on trade and only a small part of that with Western Europe — is seeking trade expansion in order to dump our goods on this continent. Trade expansion will help us all. The experience of the Common Market — like the experience of the German Zollverein — shows an increased rise in business activity and general prosperity resulting for all participants in such trade agreements, with no member profiting at the expense of another. As they say on my own Cape Cod, a rising tide lifts all the boats. And a partnership, by definition, serves both partners, without domination or unfair advantage.

Together we have been partners in adversity — let us also be partners in prosperity.

Beyond development and trade is monetary policy. Here again our interests run together. Indeed there is no field in which the wider interest of all more clearly outweighs the narrow interest of one. We have lived by that principle, as bankers to freedom, for a generation. Now that other nations — including West Germany — have found new economic strength, it is time for common efforts here, too. The great free nations of the world must take control of our monetary problems if those problems are not to take control of us.

Third and finally: Our partnership depends on common *political* purpose. Against the hazards of division and lassitude, no lesser force will serve. History tells us that disunity and relaxation are the great internal dangers of an alliance. Thucydides reported that the Peloponnesians and their allies were mighty in battle but handicapped by their policy-making body — in which, he related

each presses its own ends . . . which generally results in no action at all . . . they devote more time to the prosecution of their own purposes than to the consideration of the general welfare — each supposes that no harm will come of his own neglect, that it is the business of another to do this or that — and so, as each separately entertains the same illusion, the common cause imperceptibly decays.

Is this also to be the story of the Grand Alliance? Welded in a moment of imminent danger, will it disintegrate into complacency, with each member pressing its own ends to the neglect of the common cause? This must not be the case. Our old dangers are not gone beyond return, and any division among us would bring them back in doubled strength.

Our defenses are now strong — but they must be made stronger. Our economic goals are now clear — but we must get on with their performance. And the greatest of our necessities, the most notable of our omissions, is progress toward unity of political purpose.

For we live in a world in which our own united strength will and must be our first reliance. As I have said before, and will say again, we work toward the day when there may be real peace between us and the Communists. We will not be second in that effort. But that day is not yet here.

We in the United States and Canada are 200 million, and here on the European side of the Atlantic alliance are nearly 300 million more. The strength and unity of this half-billion human beings are and will continue to be the anchor of all freedom, for all nations. Let us from time to time pledge ourselves again to our common purpose. But let us go on, from words to actions, to intensify our efforts for still greater unity among us, to build new associations and institutions on those already established. Lofty words cannot construct an alliance or maintain it — only concrete deeds can do that.

The great present task of construction is here on this continent where the effort for a unified free Europe is under way. It is not for Americans to prescribe to Europeans how this effort should be carried forward. Nor do I believe that there is any one right course or any single final pattern. It is Europeans who are building Europe.

Yet the reunion of Europe, as Europeans shape it — bringing a permanent end to the civil wars that have repeatedly wracked the world — will continue to have the determined support of the United States. For that reunion is a necessary step in strengthening the community of freedom. It would strengthen our alliance for its defense. And it would be in our national interest as well as yours.

It is only a fully cohesive Europe that can protect us all against the fragmentation of our alliance. Only such a Europe will permit full reciprocity of treatment across the ocean, in facing the Atlantic agenda. With only such a Europe can we have a full give-and-take between equals, an equal sharing of responsibilities, and an equal level of sacrifice. I repeat again — so that there may be no misunderstanding — the choice of paths to the unity of Europe is a choice which Europe must make. But as you continue this great effort, undeterred by either difficulty or delay, you should know that this new European greatness will be not an object of fear, but a source of strength, for the United States of America.

There are other political tasks before us. We must all learn to practice more completely the art of consultation on matters stretching well beyond immediate military and economic questions. Together, for example, we must explore the possibilities of leashing the tensions of the cold war and reducing the dangers of the arms race. Together we must work to strengthen the spirit of those Europeans who are now not free, to reestablish their old ties to freedom and the West, so that their desire for liberty and their sense of nationhood and their sense of belonging to the Western Community over hundreds of years will survive for future expression. We ask those who would be our adversaries to understand that in our relations with them we will not bargain one nation's interest against another's and that the commitment to the cause of freedom is common to us all.

All of us in the West must be faithful to our conviction that peace in Europe can never be complete until everywhere in Europe, and that includes Germany,

men can choose, in peace and freedom, how their countries shall be governed, and choose — without threat to any neighbor — reunification with their countrymen.

I preach no easy liberation and I make no empty promises; but my countrymen, since our country was founded, believe strongly in the proposition that all men shall be free and all free men shall have this right of choice.

As we look steadily eastward in the hope and purpose of new freedom, we must also look — and evermore closely — to our trans-Atlantic ties. The Atlantic Community will not soon become a single overarching superstate. But practical steps toward stronger common purpose are well within our means. As we widen our common effort in defense, and our threefold cooperation in economics, we shall inevitably strengthen our political ties as well. Just as your current efforts for unity in Europe will produce a stronger voice in the dialog between us, so in America our current battle for the liberty and prosperity of all of our citizens can only deepen the meaning of our common historic purposes. In the far future there may be a great new union for us all. But for the present, there is plenty for all to do in building new and enduring connections.

In short, the words of Thucydides are a warning, not a prediction. We have it in us, as 18 years have shown, to build our defenses, to strengthen our economies, and to tighten our political bonds, both in good weather and in bad. We can move forward with the confidence that is born of success and the skill that is born of experience. And as we move, let us take heart from the certainty that we are united not only by danger and necessity, but by hope and purpose as well.

For we know now that freedom is

more than the rejection of tyranny — that prosperity is more than an escape from want — that partnership is more than a sharing of power. These are, above all, great human adventures. They must have meaning and conviction and purpose — and because they do, in your country now and in mine, in all the nations of the alliance, we are called to a great new mission.

It is not a mission of self-defense alone — for that is a means, not an end. It is not a mission of arbitrary power — for we reject the idea of one nation dominating another. The mission is to create a new social order, founded on liberty and justice, in which men are the masters of their fate, in which states are the servants of their citizens, and in which all men and women can share a better life for themselves and their children. That is the object of our common policy.

To realize this vision, we must seek a world of peace — a world in which peoples dwell together in mutual respect and work together in mutual regard — a world where peace is not a mere interlude between wars, but an incentive to

the creative energies of humanity. We will not find such a peace today, or even tomorrow. The obstacles to hope are large and menacing. Yet the goal of a peaceful world — today and tomorrow — must shape our decisions and inspire our purposes.

So we are all idealists. We are all visionaries. Let it not be said of this Atlantic generation that we left ideals and visions to the past, nor purpose and determination to our adversaries. We have come too far, we have sacrificed too much, to disdain the future now. And we shall ever remember what Goethe told us — that the "highest wisdom, the best that mankind ever knew" was the realization that "he only earns his freedom and existence who daily conquers them anew."

[NOTE: The President spoke at 4:30 p.m. before an invited audience. His opening words referred to Dr. Eugen Gerstenmaier, President of the Bundestag; Dr. Kurt-Georg Kiesinger, President of the Bundesrat and Minister-President of Württemberg-Baden; Dr. Ludwig Erhard, Vice Chancellor and Minister of Economics; Dr. Georg August Zinn, Minister-President of Hesse; and Werner Bockelmann, Mayor of Frankfurt. Author's note.]

Ronald Steel: THE END OF THE POSTWAR WORLD

Ronald Steel, a former Foreign Service officer, has been a frequent contributor to journals of national and international affairs. Looking back at the 1950's he saw the frenzied international activities of Acheson and Dulles as the reverse side of isolationism, from total irresponsibility to total responsibility. NATO was likened to a crusade, and any defection from our allies represented heresy. Steel asked that America recognize that Europe has recovered and wishes to remove herself from the wardship implied in NATO. "The old order has broken up."

AMERICA began her involvement in the moral fate of the world only in 1945, and then with considerable reluctance. The collapse of the old order made the United States the most powerful nation on earth, endowing her by default with the ability to shape the order that was emerging. But it was a responsibility that most Americans greeted with mixed feelings. The United States had been too long shut off from the world, too long protected from the unpleasantness that goes with military power. During our period of isolationism we bred a political puritanism, seeing in the discordant ambitions of other nations a field of dishonor unworthy of our ideals.

When we were finally thrown into the political arena by the postwar power vacuum, this inbred moralism turned outward. We thought we could settle the problems of the world with the same energy and dedication that had allowed us to win the war. We came not to influence but to transform, a crusader rather than a teacher. Although we did not crave power, we learned to accept it as the means by which the virtues we practiced at home — free speech and free enterprise — could become the new world order. From a grudging acceptance of political involvement, we came to prize our military and economic strength as an instrument that gave us great power over the affairs of others.

The old formula of isolationism was turned upside down as we rushed to embrace our new global responsibilities. Seized by a passion for pacts and resolutions, we saw in these international contracts an instrument for imposing order on a world grown turbulent and unpredictable. Dubious alliances, many of them held together only by the verbiage of the conferences that spawned them, were hastily erected to give legal framework to our new involvement. "We began with a quest for bases," as Stillman and Pfaff have commented,

but before it was over we were supplying arms, economic support, and military guarantees on every continent. Having failed to examine precisely what we wanted from each of these alliances beyond a mere profession of allegiance to our cause, we gave military arrangements without political warrant and justified political pacts with military arguments.

Consumed by our rivalry with the Soviet Union, we poured our wealth and our arms into every corner of the globe, imagining that tanks and treaties could make democracy triumphant in the world. Intimidated by the pretensions of communist ideology, and transfixed by the heady vision of universal responsibility, we saw a vital American interest in every street riot and palace squabble around the earth's vast periphery. Since we had made ourselves the overseers of every nation's moral destiny, it is not surprising that we were sometimes deceived and often disappointed. By reducing the complexities of world politics to the struggle of "freedom" against "communism," we made it inevitable that we were used by those who had little interest in our ideals, but a great deal to gain from our competition with the Russians. In Edmund Wilson's words:

Our national mission, if our budget proves anything, has taken on colossal dimensions, but in its interference in foreign countries and its support of oppressive regimes, it has hardly been a liberating mission, and the kind of idealism involved is becoming insane and intolerant.

American diplomacy during the 1950s was simply a reflection of our national style: a morality codified in corporation law and the Old Testament. Its architect, John Foster Dulles, was not the instigator but merely the embodiment of this legal Calvinism. But an idealism chained to a nonexistent international morality usually turns to indignation and ultimately cynicism. Frustration is the great undoer of all virtues. It was only natural that our diplomacy should have reflected our impatience with a world in which evil mysteriously remained a constant element of man's behavior. Having been born to freedom rather than forced constantly to rewin it, we Americans have developed a natural repugnance to the imperfectibility and periodic malevolence of man. With our own history as a guide, it seemed reasonable to assume that moral perfectibility could be legislated, or if need be imposed, upon less fortunate peoples once the wisdom of our institutions was made evident.

The scope of this ambition was matched only by its fantasy. Time and again it foundered on the realities of an amoral world. Mocked in our generosity, we turned from meddling do-goodism to self-righteousness. The power rivalry with Russia became a moral crusade for the allegiance of mankind. He who was not with us was against us; he who would not accept our vision of the world was blind; he who would seek neutrality from the ideological struggles of the cold war was immoral. Baffled by a world in which allies could become adversaries, and where the struggle for power was unending, American diplomacy reverted to the spirit of the wartime crusade: a time when total victory provided the password for fighting the war, and when the image of total evil justified the use of the atomic bomb. No longer simply "the carrying out of policy by other means," as von Clausewitz believed, war in our time has become a moral cause. As Kenneth Thompson has observed:

Nations find themselves today in a situation not too dissimilar from that obtaining domestically within the United States prior to the Civil War. The sanctities of religion and science are invoked to show that one course of action, one nation's program, will execute a divine mandate. Nations go to war not in dispute over territorial boundaries but to make the world safe for democracy or to destroy human wickedness incarnated in evil men like Hitler and Mussolini. Wars of righteousness in which compromise and limited objectives are looked on as treason are today's counterpart of earlier historical wars of religion.

But with total war made irrational by modern weapons, absolute righteousness eventually becomes absolutely irrelevant. Faced by the decline of ideologies and the collapse of old alliances, we have begun to recognize that our dominion is not divinely inspired, and that the American image cannot be imposed upon an infinitely complex world. Our idealism has faded and with it our innocence. "We must face the fact," President Kennedy said candidly,

that the United States is neither omnipotent nor omniscient, that we cannot always impose our will on the other 94 per cent of mankind, that we cannot right every wrong or reverse each adversity, and that therefore there cannot be an American solution for every world problem.

It is a wise judgment, but one which has yet to be applied.

The passing of American omnipotence has not been easy to accept. There are those among us, confused by the conflicting values and limited choices of the contemporary world, who find in political irrationality the relief for their moral indignation. Declaring themselves the prime interpreters of American patriotism, they rage against the paradoxes of a world dominated by nuclear terror, rabid nationalism, and incessant change, seeking to impose a mold of conformity upon a plural society swept by forces outside its control. Yearning for the simplicity of the old order, they would master change by denying its existence, defend democracy by adopting the methods of totalitarianism. In their minds there is no conflict between the values of American democracy and the inroads of the "military-industrial complex," as General Eisenhower termed it, upon the structure of our society, for they see democracy as simply the extension of American military power.

They are, in a sense, the last of the romantics, holding desperately to the moral certitude that allows them to deny complexities they prefer to ignore. Having committed themselves to the ideological battles of the cold war, they find it intolerable to believe that the old labels, like the old causes, no longer explain the world as it is. In their naïve reactions to the pretensions of communist theory, they express, in an extreme manner, our fatal fascination with ideologies. Paying homage to our native pragmatism, we are vaguely suspicious of intellectual theories and master plans. But when these theories are embodied in an ideology — whether it be the "American way of life" or the "world communist conspiracy" — we become transfixed by the verbiage that surrounds them. Having digested the theories, we cling to them tenaciously even after the conditions that created them have ceased to exist. "Our American policy," as Louis Halle has commented,

has been based on the situation as it appeared to exist in the period immediately after the war. Because we have invested in that policy not only our resources, but so much of our emotional and intellectual energy as well, and because such powerful vested interests depend on it, our whole disposition is to cling to the unchanging nominal image in preference to the unstable reality.

Just as the myth of free enterprise persists in an age when capitalism could not survive without government regulation, government subsidies, and government encouragement, so the myth of "international communism" lingers on even though it is ceasing to be international or even particularly communistic.

By confounding Marxist scripture with blueprints for Soviet action, we have been overimpressed by the lip service Russian leaders pay to the theology of nineteenth-century communist doctrines. We tend to be more carried away by their ideology than they are themselves, endowing their liturgical chants with a weight out of all proportion to their true significance. Seeing communism as a religious faith, we imagined that there could be no differences among communists, irrespective of their nationality or cultural history. We forgot that the bloodiest wars of European history were fought among nations professing a common faith, that wars of religion, like civil wars, are the most brutal and uncompromising. Because we were overwhelmed by the verbiage of communist dogma instead of concerning ourselves with the realities of national power, we persisted for a decade and a half in our refusal to recognize that a communist Russia might find itself at odds with a communist China.

Yet, if we shed our ideological blinkers, it is apparent that in their pursuit of national security today's Russian commissars share many of the same objectives as yesterday's czars: to ring the western frontier with a cordon of buffer states, to contain Germany, and to block any hostile power from dominating the Continent. Within Europe, Russia has

been as much a defensive as an imperial-
ist power, finding in her occupation of
eastern Europe the means by which she
could assure her security. Emerging from
the war as the dominant power of Eurasia
and determined to forge a commanding
place for herself in a world where the
old power balance had been destroyed
and a new one not yet formed, Russia
equated her own economic and political
interests with the gospel of communism.
Marxist ideology became a necessary
rationalization for actions the Russians
would have taken in any case: setting up
friendly regimes in the satellites, and
keeping Germany divided. While the
United States wanted to restore the old
European power balance under the
watchful eye of the United Nations, the
Russians were determined to build a new
one. It is not surprising that these two
great powers should have clashed head-
on at the end of the war. They were
dedicated to conflicting views of the
world.

But now, some two decades later,
Russia, at last recovered from the war
and liberated from her Stalinist night-
mare, has become a technologically
advanced and increasingly bourgeois
society, dedicated to the new status quo
and desperately trying to preserve it in
the face of Chinese militantism. It is now
the Kremlin that urges "peaceful coexistence" rather than world revolution,
and is willing to support wars of "national liberation" only so long as they do
not threaten Russia's own national interests. Russia, to be sure, remains a threat
to the West whose temptations to military adventurism must still be kept under
control by a powerful Western deterrent. We can expect the Kremlin to seek
the spread of communism by whatever
means may be open to it. But as they
demonstrated by pulling their missiles

out of Cuba in 1962, the Russians have
no intention of sacrificing their own security to the support of foreign communists. As the revolution devours its children, so its grandchildren devour the
revolution. Unwilling to risk all to win
the world because they have too much
to lose, Soviet leaders have not hesitated
to make it clear that the world revolution takes a back seat to the protection
of the Soviet state. Rich in a world of
poverty, conservative in a fraternity of
revolutionaries, today's Russia has become a self-protective state hesitant to
rock the international boat too greatly.
As the world's leading imperial power,
possessed of lands seized by force in Asia
and eastern Europe, Russia espouses "national liberation" only at her own peril.

As Russians savor the pleasures of re-
frigerators and television, an impover-
ished China has inherited the mantle of
world revolution. Desperate in its poverty, contemptuous of a Western culture
it has traditionally deemed inferior, resentful of Russian prosperity and embit-
tered by the refusal of Soviet "comrades"
to share their wealth and their atomic
bombs, Peking is determined to seize the
leadership of the communist world from
Moscow. Speaking for the ideological
fanatics of all nations and for the poverty-
stricken two-thirds of the world which
has little to lose but its hunger, China
proclaims itself the champion of the new
revolution. Charging each other with
various forms of heresy, the two communist giants labor over the texts of Marx
and Lenin in search of invectives to
justify their own national ambitions. Like
medieval scholastics, they conduct theo-
logical quarrels over fine points of scripture, arguing who is more faithful to the
spirit of St. Marx, or how many underdeveloped nations can dance on the head
of a loan from Western "imperialists."

Despite the dreams of Marx, communism has proved to be no substitute for nationalism. Like any dogma, it demands the supreme authority to interpret and enforce its doctrine. But, as Edward Crankshaw has pointed out:

The moment the authority of this supreme headquarters is challenged, the whole chain of command collapses. It is not simply a question of, in this particular instance, Peking challenging Moscow. Once Peking has been allowed to challenge Moscow successfully, the magic spell has been broken. Other parties, with problems very different from the problems of Peking and Moscow, feel free to issue their own challenges.

Under pressure from communist nationalists and "revisionists" from Romania to Cuba, Moscow has been forced to play the role of headmaster in a school of squabbling students — still able to exert its authority on crucial questions of foreign policy, but no longer able to control the nuances of internal life in the satellites. The communist "monolith," which everyone a few years ago thought to be as solid and unyielding as Stalin's monument in Prague (now vanished and unlamented), has become an armed camp of political squabbles, economic rivalries, and internecine feuds. Khrushchev turns to Tito, the dark prince of heresy, in his disputes with Mao; the Poles lend their support to Moscow in foreign affairs, but only at the price of gaining greater freedom to pursue their own internal affairs; and the Bulgarians shop around for trade deals with the West. Even that old archrival of the Kremlin, the Catholic Church, under the reconciliatory policies initiated by Pope John XXIII and continued by Paul VI, is winning a new freedom for its functions in eastern Europe — a freedom that may have a significant effect in breaking down some of the barriers be-

tween the two Europes. Belgrade, Warsaw, and Budapest are no longer cities trapped in an alien empire, but outposts of change in an eastern Europe that is demanding the freedom to follow its own path to communism. With priests, motor scooters, and modern jazz spreading across the satellites, the cracks in the iron curtain have begun to widen.

The fundamental fact of the postwar world — the East-West confrontation between America and her allies and the Soviet Union and her satellites — has become insufficient to explain the complex rivalries and subtle antagonisms that are so dominant today. The monolithic communist bloc, which lasted for more than a decade after Yugoslavia's defection in 1948, has been so rent by gaps and fissures that there is little prospect of its unity's being restored. But at the same time, the Western alliance, which was created to contain that communist monolith, has been subject to the same stresses and is experiencing a similar disarray. Both parts of Europe have responded to the breakup of the old order by outspoken demands to emerge from under the shadow of their protectors. There has been a revival of nationalism that has made the old alliances, like the old formulas that divided the world into two irreconcilable parts, seem anachronistic, and perhaps even irrelevant.

While we applaud the schisms within the communist world as inevitable, the disarray of the North Atlantic Treaty Organization — symbolized in the defiance of Gaullist France but rooted in the assertiveness of a prosperous Europe — strikes us as unnatural. Having committed our lives and our fortunes to the alliance with western Europe, it strikes us as an incomprehensible heresy that the Europeans seem to be turning their backs upon America. This dismay would not be so great were our enthusiasm for the alliance not so unbounded. Ever since its creation in 1949 the Atlantic pact has been the object of a remarkable veneration. Our entire diplomacy revolves around it; it is the one constant in a sea of shifting values and allegiances. NATO has been more than simply one military alliance among many; it has entered our popular mythology, enshrined in the hagiography of the cold war. It has become a kind of passion, the one subject on which liberals and conservatives, management and labor, one-worlders and the radical right are able to agree. As the Crusades were to medieval Christianity, so NATO has been to American diplomacy under three administrations: the instrument by which all incongruities would be subsumed in the quest for a higher moral order.

The alliance with western Europe — our friends, but more realistically, our wards — became sanctified as the very symbol of American power. There was nothing base in these feelings, nor was there anything base in the actions that flowed from them. On the contrary, America showed a remarkable forgiveness toward its former enemies and a magnanimity toward its allies. But in building the new alliance with Europe, we also assumed, unsurprisingly perhaps, our own omnipotence. Possessing a virtual monopoly of economic and military power within the West, the United States could not refrain from exercising the prerogatives of this heady power. However natural this may have been, it did not receive the enthusiastic acclaim of our European allies. Their weakness allowed us to assume undiluted approval of our personality and our policies; in reality it was only a grudging acquiescence that they were determined to remedy at the earliest opportunity.

With characteristic candor General de Gaulle described in his war memoirs the impression that powerful America made upon a war-weakened Europe:

The United States, delighting in her resources, feeling that she had within herself insufficient scope for her energies, wishing to help those who were in misery or bondage the world over, yielded in her turn to that taste for intervention in which the instinct for domination cloaked itself.

Hardly a flattering judgment, and perhaps not even a fair one, it revealed the resentment over the postwar American directorate that seethed beneath Europe's acknowledgment of her own abject dependence.

So long as communist militants threatened to take over their unstable governments from within, the Europeans clung to America for support. So long as the Red Army seemed poised to sweep from the Elbe to the Channel, they were grateful for American protection. But as the panic of the early 1950s passed and the Russian peril seemed to diminish, the alliance began to lose the sense of urgency which had originally inspired it. Without the Russian bear breathing down their necks, the Europeans no longer found it important to take their NATO goals seriously. Fearful that the alliance forged with such difficulty might fall apart in the wake of the first Russian thaw, Washington had to create ever bigger bogeymen to frighten our allies. Thus we argued that the disaffection of Yugoslavia, the death of Stalin, the revolt in Poland and Hungary changed nothing, unless it made the Russian peril even more terrible.

Every Soviet action was treated not in terms of its effect upon the world power balance, but upon its significance for NATO. If the Russians appeared to falter, it was only to catch the West napping. If they blundered, it was to confuse us. If they compromised, it was only to seduce us. We could not imagine that they had our moral failings; and if they did, we could not admit it lest NATO disappear as a result. Having persuaded ourselves that the defense of Europe was our obligation even more than it was a European obligation, we became suitors to our allies: beseeching them to allow us the privilege of protecting them. The very possibility of a mellowing of Russian ambitions summoned the most horrendous prospects in official Washington. Built on alarm and nourished by emergency, NATO developed a vested interest in the perpetuation of that very state of emergency.

Unfortunately for diplomatic strategists, time does not stand still. Dictators die, nations rise and decline, ideologies fade, new rivalries emerge, and every revolution has its *Thermidor*. The world today is quite different from that of the late 1940s. Two events of far-reaching significance have altered the old power balance. The first is the revolution in weaponry which has made the United States, for the first time in history, directly vulnerable to devastation at the hands of its enemies; the second is the construction of an economically powerful and politically aggressive Europe. Together they have crumbled the old foundation of NATO and made its future appear dubious, and perhaps even undesirable.

The military disputes which perennially shake NATO, the arguments as to who shall be permitted to have a trigger finger on the Bomb, and who shall die in the defense of whose interests, is only part of the problem of the totally new relationship that now exists between America and Europe. For more than half a century we have taken it for granted that a feuding, divided Europe must be dependent upon the United States to bolster its inefficient economy and settle its internecine wars. Forced to come to the aid of Europe twice during a single generation, we found it easier, and probably safer, to take charge of Europe's problems ourselves rather than to risk again being called in at the last minute to settle yet another war on the most disadvantageous terms. Having accepted the responsibility for the defense of Europe at a time when the Europeans were obviously too weak to defend themselves, we came to assume that both the Soviet menace and European weakness were permanent fixtures of the postwar world. NATO — which was designed as an extraordinary commitment for a specific situation, a commitment that involved great dangers for the United States — became an ingrained dogma of American foreign policy.

The Europeans, as the price of their weakness — caused, to be sure, by the folly of their own civil wars — accepted American generals who gave them orders, and American diplomats who decided what their foreign policy should be. But as the Soviet menace diminished, so did their gratitude and enthusiasm for American protection. Spurred by their remarkable economic recovery, the Europeans have become increasingly self-confident and resentful of the American leadership that they had formerly been willing to tolerate. With the passing of their economic dependency on the United States has come a desire to play a more independent role in the world and perhaps even to dispense with the American protection which they had once solicited as the only guarantee of their security.

Whatever fears the Europeans may have had of a Russian invasion now seem to have largely disappeared. Even during the panic generated by the Korean war we overestimated that fear, for it was not the Red Army the Europeans feared so much as the internal weakness of their own societies that might invite communist-inspired *coups* which the Russians, in turn, would move to support — as in the case of Czechoslovakia. If fifteen years ago the alliance with America was the guarantee of their survival, today it has become a mixed blessing, if not a handicap. More likely than a Russian invasion, to their mind, is a nuclear war between America and Russia in which Europe would be the unwilling third party and eventual corpse. If there is any chance for them to escape destruction in such a war, it would not seem to be improved by a military alliance with the United States or by American soldiers and bases on their soil. The Cuban crisis of 1962 simply lent support to what was already a growing belief among many Europeans that Europe's future lies not in her remaining a partner to America in the Atlantic alliance but in becoming a Third Force standing somewhere between the two thermonuclear giants.

While the United States remains consumed by the cold-war struggle with Soviet Russia, pumping more than half its national budget into defense, neglecting its own internal needs, and making its industry dependent on military contracts, the Europeans have acted as though the cold war, for all practical purposes, were already over. While young Americans are subject to a two-year draft, most European nations have cut theirs to eighteen months or one year, and Britain has eliminated conscription completely. While the United States suffers a chronic drain in its balance of payments in order to finance its foreign-aid burden and station an army of four hundred thousand men in Europe, our NATO allies show little interest in easing our burden: Britain refrains from increasing her land forces on the Conti-

nent, Germany prefers to keep the riches of her *Wirtschaftswunder* rather than share it with the underdeveloped nations, and Gaullist France refuses even to co-operate with the NATO command in strategic planning. While United States research skills go into atomic weapons and space bonanzas, the Europeans have been busily modernizing their industries and today are outpacing America in the very fields in which we were once predominant. As we fret over trade restrictions and embargoes for iron-curtain countries, the Europeans have tripled their trade with the Soviet bloc in the past ten years and are eagerly signing contracts giving them access to the expanding markets of the East.

The Atlantic alliance, which has been the keystone of American foreign policy during three administrations, has begun to founder under the impact of Europe's new nationalism and the apparent decline of the Russian military threat. There is no longer any agreement on how NATO shall be organized, where it is going, or even what its purposes are. Britain and France defy the Pentagon's demands for a nuclear monopoly, Germany blocks any accord that would ease the tension over Berlin, Italy flirts with a popular front that would bring communists into the government, Portugal places her African empire above her ties to NATO, Norway and Denmark refuse to accept American atomic weapons on their soil, Turkey and Greece depend on American military aid to bolster their economies and keep order among their people, Canada seethes with resentment under the American shadow, and Iceland has told the United States that there no longer seems to be any need for an air base there.

Despite Washington's ringing appeals for "Atlantic unity," a defiant France has struck a deep chord of response in its efforts to cut Europe loose from the United States. Even Britain feels conflicting interests as she tries to reconcile her yearning for the old "special relationship" with America with her determination not be locked out of Europe. And in a class apart lies Germany, dependent upon America for her protection but upon her European neighbors for her economic existence, eager to have a voice commensurate with her growing power but hesitant to choose, vacillating between caution and boldness; Germany, haunted by the specters of the past, and caught by the temptation to play once again a dominant role between East and West.

This disarray within the alliance is more than simply a dispute among allies as to the proper means toward a commonly desired end. It is the ends themselves which are now in question. The problem facing the Atlantic alliance today is not so much how it shall protect Europe from Russian invasion — an invasion that virtually no one now believes in — but what kind of political settlement will be made between Russia and the West in Europe. The collapse of Atlantic unity is merely the result of the transformation of the old military impasse into a period of diplomatic fluidity where Europe's political future is at stake. There are many along the Potomac and elsewhere who imagine that Europe's new resistance to American leadership is a kind of cultural lag that will evaporate as soon as General de Gaulle, its most fervent advocate, departs from the scene. But for all their ardor, those who believe that America and Europe must be forever linked in common purpose give too much credit to de Gaulle and not enough to those men all over the Continent who are building the new Europe. A Europe resistant to American direction is not a personal idiosyncrasy of Charles de

Gaulle, but rather the result of twenty years of European recovery.

This is why de Gaulle's departure is unlikely to bring back the good old days of transatlantic unity, a unity always more apparent than real since it rested on the great disparity of American power over European. Rather, it is likely to mean only its dispersion to less articulate, but no less passionate, advocates of European nationalism. The new leaders of Germany do not necessarily share Chancellor Adenauer's unflinching Atlantic loyalties or his bitter intransigence toward the East. Britain oscillates between its reluctance to join forces with Europe and its persistent refusal to remain totally dependent on America by giving up its nuclear deterrent. And in France, where the opposition on the left has polarized around a new alliance between communists and socialists, the prospect of a popular front is hardly any more promising for Atlantic unity than Gaullism has been. Instead of posing a temporary detour to the "grand design" of Atlantic partnership, de Gaulle seems to be the spokesman for the nationalism that has become the hallmark of the new Europe.

The distress and confusion that have come in the wake of this new attitude among our allies is only the expression of far deeper changes in the international order. Our policies remain frozen in the vocabulary of a postwar world which has ceased to exist. That period when Russia and America could each presume to speak for half of mankind, when there were few neutrals and the struggle between the "free world" and the "communist monolith" seemed the only political reality — all this has now begun to pass into history. Its pretensions have come to seem arrogant and its narrowness self-defeating. The vast military power by which the two nuclear giants once dominated their allies and intimidated each other has not been able to preserve their dominion or even serve their vital interests. The atomic bomb, by making war the instrument of absolute destruction, has also made it absolutely irrational. The United States, having become a great world power at a time when military force was losing its importance, is now faced with the problem of protecting its interests without being able to use the weapons on which its power rests.

While neither Russia nor America is particularly happy with the present nuclear stalemate, they have begun to recognize that they share a peculiar community of interests. Their present rivalry is not a stable one — it keeps breaking down, despite their desire to restrain it, in unmanageable places like Cuba and Indochina — but they know that the alternative is far worse: a world in which their radioactive ruins would be fought over by an expansionist China and an ambitious Europe. Russia's great rival today in the churning *tiers monde* of poor and backward states is not America, with whom she shares a tiresome foreign-aid burden and a boring balance of terror, but a militant China which threatens to steal her revolutionary thunder — and with it the leadership of world communism. Similarly, the United States, plagued by a sluggish economy, an enormous arms budget, and unwieldy surpluses, is under increasing challenge from an economically aggressive European community with uncertain political ambitions. The nuclear test ban of 1963 was the recognition of this community of interests, for it provided the superpowers with a mutually desirable instrument to discourage the spread of atomic weapons and thereby preserve their own

military pre-eminence. As Russia turned its back on China, so the United States joined its old rival to block national nuclear arsenals in Europe.

Events have drawn us beyond the postwar world into a perplexing period of transition whose rules we have not yet learned and whose rivalries we do not yet understand. Gaullism has shocked our sensibilities because it is based upon the assumption that the cold war is virtually over and that the alliances forged to wage it have now become obsolete. Starting from this, it goes on to build a diplomacy for the new Europe and the new political conditions that have emerged. De Gaulle did not invent these new conditions, but he is acting on the belief that all the old emotional baggage of the past twenty years — containment, bipolarity, the communist bloc, the division of Europe, and the NATO alliance — are now irrelevant. In the face of this challenge, as Walter Lippmann has written, we are a nation

which has to reappraise, revise, and readjust policies put together during a half century of European dependence on the wealth and power of the United States. In the world today, the United States is on its own to a degree which no man now in the United States government has ever known before.

The old order has broken up. We have reached the end of a postwar world whose premises were based on terror, but whose conditions had become familiar, and even comforting, over the years. The waters we are entering are uncharted and perhaps treacherous, and we are not likely to steer safely through them unless we have the courage to question the old assumptions which once seemed eternal and have now become so threadbare.

J. William Fulbright: MYTHS ABOUT COMMUNISM

*In a major speech before the Senate in 1964, the Chairman of the
Senate Foreign Relations Committee, Senator J. William Fulbright of
Arkansas, exhorted Americans to look at realities, to forsake myths.
Europe had changed since 1949; Communism had changed since 1949.
"The myth is that every Communist State is an unmitigated evil and a
relentless enemy of the free world; the reality is that some Communist
regimes pose a threat to the free world while others pose little or none."
Without saying that NATO should dissolve, he implied that its military
organization had lost its mission.*

MR. FULBRIGHT. Mr. President, there is an inevitable divergence, attributable to the imperfections of the human mind, between the world as it is and the world as men perceive it. As long as our perceptions are reasonably close to objective reality, it is possible for us to act upon our problems in a rational and appropriate manner. But when our perceptions fail to keep pace with events, when we refuse to believe something because it displeases or frightens us, or because it is simply startlingly unfamiliar, then the gap between fact and perception becomes a chasm, and action becomes irrelevant and irrational.

There has always — and inevitably — been some divergence between the realities of foreign policy and our ideas about it. This divergence has in certain respects been growing, rather than narrowing; and we are handicapped, accordingly, by policies based on old myths, rather than current realities. This divergence is, in my opinion, dangerous and unnecessary — dangerous, because it can reduce foreign policy to a fraudulent game of imagery and appearances; unnecessary, because it can be overcome by the determination of men in high office to dispel prevailing misconceptions by the candid dissemination of unpleasant, but inescapable, facts.

Before commenting on some of the specific areas where I believe our policies are at least partially based on cherished myths, rather than objective facts, I should like to suggest two possible reasons for the growing divergence between the realities and our perceptions of current world politics. The first is the radical change in relations between and within the Communist and the free world; and the second is the tendency of too many of us to confuse means with ends and, accordingly, to adhere to prevailing practices with a fervor befitting immutable principles.

Although it is too soon to render a definitive judgment, there is mounting evidence that events of recent years have wrought profound changes in the character of East-West relations. In the Cuban missile crisis of October 1962, the United States proved to the Soviet Union that a policy of aggression and adventure involved unacceptable risks. In the signing of the test ban treaty, each side in effect assured the other that it was prepared to forego, at least for the present, any bid for a decisive military or political breakthrough. These occurrences, it

From J. William Fulbright, "Old Myths and New Realities," *Congressional Record, U. S. Senate,
88th Congress, 2nd Session* (Washington: U. S. Government Printing Office, 1964), pp. 6227–6229.

should be added, took place against the background of the clearly understood strategic superiority — but not supremacy — of the United States.

It seems reasonable, therefore, to suggest that the character of the cold war has, for the present, at least, been profoundly altered: by the drawing back of the Soviet Union from extremely aggressive policies; by the implicit repudiation by both sides of a policy of "total victory"; and by the establishment of an American strategic superiority which the Soviet Union appears to have tacitly accepted because it has been accompanied by assurances that it will be exercised by the United States with responsibility and restraint. These enormously important changes may come to be regarded by historians as the foremost achievements of the Kennedy administration in the field of foreign policy. Their effect has been to commit us to a foreign policy which can accurately — though perhaps not prudently — be defined as one of "peaceful coexistence."

Another of the results of the lowering of tensions between East and West is that each is now free to enjoy the luxury of accelerated strife and squabbling within its own domain. The ideological thunderbolts between Washington and Moscow which until a few years ago seemed a permanent part of our daily lives have become a pale shadow of their former selves. Now, instead, the United States waits in fascinated apprehension for the Olympian pronouncements that issue from Paris at 6-month intervals while the Russians respond to the crude epithets of Peiping with almost plaintive rejoinders about "those who want to start a war against everybody."

These astonishing changes in the configuration of the postwar world have had an unsettling effect on both public and official opinion in the United States. One reason for this, I believe, lies in the fact that we are a people used to looking at the world, and indeed at ourselves, in moralistic rather than empirical terms. We are predisposed to regard any conflict as a clash between good and evil rather than as simply a clash between conflicting interests. We are inclined to confuse freedom and democracy, which we regard as moral principles, with the way in which they are practiced in America — with capitalism, federalism, and the two-party system, which are not moral principles but simply the preferred and accepted practices of the American people. There is much cant in American moralism and not a little inconsistency. It resembles in some ways the religious faith of the many respectable people who, in Samuel Butler's words, "would be equally horrified to hear the Christian religion doubted or to see it practiced."

Our national vocabulary is full of "self-evident truths" not only about "life, liberty, and happiness," but about a vast number of personal and public issues, including the cold war. It has become one of the "self-evident truths" of the postwar era that just as the President resides in Washington and the Pope in Rome, the Devil resides immutably in Moscow. We have come to regard the Kremlin as the permanent seat of his power and we have grown almost comfortable with a menace which, though unspeakably evil, has had the redeeming virtues of constancy, predictability, and familiarity. Now the Devil has betrayed us by traveling abroad and, worse still, by dispersing himself, turning up now here, now there, and in many places at once, with a devilish disregard for the laboriously constructed frontiers of ideology.

We are confronted with a complex and

fluid world situation and we are not adapting ourselves to it. We are clinging to old myths in the face of new realities and we are seeking to escape the contradictions by narrowing the permissible bounds of public discussion, by relegating an increasing number of ideas and viewpoints to a growing category of "unthinkable thoughts." I believe that this tendency can and should be reversed, that it is within our ability, and unquestionably in our interests, to cut loose from established myths and to start thinking some "unthinkable thoughts" — about the cold war and East-West relations, about the underdeveloped countries and particularly those in Latin America, about the changing nature of the Chinese Communist threat in Asia and about the festering war in Vietnam.

The master myth of the cold war is that the Communist bloc is a monolith composed of governments which are not really governments at all but organized conspiracies, divided among themselves perhaps in certain matters of tactics, but all equally resolute and implacable in their determination to destroy the free world.

I believe that the Communist world is indeed hostile to the free world in its general and long-term intentions but that the existence of this animosity in principle is far less important for our foreign policy than the great variations in its intensity and character both in time and among the individual members of the Communist bloc. Only if we recognize these variations, ranging from China, which poses immediate threats to the free world, to Poland and Yugoslavia, which pose none, can we hope to act effectively upon the bloc and to turn its internal differences to our own advantage and to the advantage of those bloc countries which wish to maximize their

independence. It is the responsibility of our national leaders, both in the executive branch and in Congress, to acknowledge and act upon these realities, even at the cost of saying things which will not win immediate widespread enthusiasm.

For a start, we can acknowledge the fact that the Soviet Union, though still a most formidable adversary, has ceased to be totally and implacably hostile to the West. It has shown a new willingness to enter mutually advantageous arrangements with the West and, thus far at least, to honor them. It has, therefore, become possible to divert some of our energies from the prosecution of the cold war to the relaxation of the cold war and to deal with the Soviet Union, for certain purposes, as a normal state with normal and traditional interests.

If we are to do these things effectively, we must distinguish between communism as an ideology and the power and policy of the Soviet state. It is not communism as a doctrine, or communism as it is practiced within the Soviet Union or within any other country, that threatens us. How the Soviet Union organizes its internal life, the gods and doctrines that it worships, are matters for the Soviet Union to determine. It is not Communist dogma as espoused within Russia but Communist imperialism that threatens us and other peoples of the non-Communist world. Insofar as a great nation mobilizes its power and resources for aggressive purposes, that nation, regardless of ideology, makes itself our enemy. Insofar as a nation is content to practice its doctrines within its own frontiers, that nation, however repugnant its ideology, is one with which we have no proper quarrel. We must deal with the Soviet Union as a great power, quite apart from differences of ideology. To the extent that the Soviet leaders abandon the global ambitions of Marxist ideology, in fact if not in words, it becomes possible for us to engage in normal relations with them, relations which probably cannot be close or trusting for many years to come but which can be gradually freed of the terror and the tensions of the cold war.

In our relations with the Russians, and indeed in our relations with all nations, we would do well to remember, and to act upon, the words of Pope John in the great Encyclical, Pacem in Terris:

"It must be borne in mind," said Pope John, "that to proceed gradually is the law of life in all its expressions, therefore, in human institutions, too, it is not possible to renovate for the better except by working from within them, gradually. Violence has always achieved only destruction, not construction, the kindling of passions, not their pacification, the accumulation of hate and ruin, not the reconciliation of the contending parties. And it has reduced men and parties to the difficult task of rebuilding, after sad experience, on the ruins of discord.

Important opportunities have been created for Western policy by the development of "polycentrism" in the Communist bloc. The Communist nations, as George Kennan has pointed out, are, like the Western nations, currently caught up in a crisis of indecision about their relations with countries outside their own ideological bloc. The choices open to the satellite states are limited but by no means insignificant. They can adhere slavishly to Soviet preferences or they can strike out on their own, within limits, to enter into mutually advantageous relations with the West.

Whether they do so, and to what extent, is to some extent at least within the power of the West to determine. If we persist in the view that all Communist regimes are equally hostile and equally

threatening to the West, and that we can have no policy toward the captive nations except the eventual overthrow of their Communist regimes, then the West may enforce upon the Communist bloc a degree of unity which the Soviet Union has shown itself to be quite incapable of imposing — just as Stalin in the early postwar years frightened the West into a degree of unity that it almost certainly could not have attained by its own unaided efforts. If, on the other hand, we are willing to re-examine the view that all Communist regimes are alike in the threat which they pose for the West — a view which had a certain validity in Stalin's time — then we may be able to exert an important influence on the course of events within a divided Communist world.

We are to a great extent the victims, and the Soviets the beneficiaries, of our own ideological convictions, and of the curious contradictions which they involve. We consider it a form of subversion of the free world, for example, when the Russians enter trade relations or conclude a consular convention or establish airline connections with a free country in Asia, Africa, or Latin America — and to a certain extent we are right. On the other hand, when it is proposed that we adopt the same strategy in reverse — by extending commercial credits to Poland or Yugoslavia, or by exchanging Ambassadors with a Hungarian regime which has changed considerably in character since the revolution of 1956 — then the same patriots who are so alarmed by Soviet activities in the free world charge our policymakers with "giving aid and comfort to the enemy" and with innumerable other categories of idiocy and immorality.

It is time that we resolved this contradiction and separated myth from reality. The myth is that every Communist state is an unmitigated evil and a relentless enemy of the free world; the reality is that some Communist regimes pose a threat to the free world while others pose little or none, and that if we will recognize these distinctions, we ourselves will be able to influence events in the Communist bloc in a way favorable to the security of the free world.

It could well be argued . . . writes George Kennan —

That if the major Western Powers had full freedom of movement in devising their own policies, it would be within their power to determine whether the Chinese view, or the Soviet view, or perhaps a view more liberal than either would ultimately prevail within the Communist camp. (George Kennan, "Polycentrism and Western Policy," Foreign Affairs, January 1964, page 178.)

There are numerous areas in which we can seek to reduce the tensions of the cold war and to bring a degree of normalcy into our relations with the Soviet Union and other Communist countries — once we have resolved that it is safe and wise to do so. We have already taken important steps in this direction: the Antarctic and Austrian treaties and the nuclear test ban treaty, the broadening of East-West cultural and educational relations, and the expansion of trade.

On the basis of recent experience and present economic needs, there seems little likelihood of a spectacular increase in trade between Communist and Western countries, even if existing restrictions were to be relaxed. Free world trade with Communist countries has been increasing at a steady but unspectacular rate, and it seems unlikely to be greatly accelerated because of the limited ability of the Communist countries to pay for increased imports. A modest increase in East-West trade may nonetheless serve as a modest instrument of East-West detente — provided that we are able to overcome the myth that trade with Communist countries is a compact with the Devil and to recognize that, on the contrary, trade can serve as an effective and honorable means of advancing both peace and human welfare.

Whether we are able to make these philosophic adjustments or not, we cannot escape the fact that our efforts to devise a common Western trade policy are a palpable failure and that our allies are going to trade with the Communist bloc whether we like it or not. The world's major exporting nations are slowly but steadily increasing their trade with the Communist bloc and the bloc countries are showing themselves to be reliable customers. Since 1958 Western Europe has been increasing its exports to the East at the rate of about 7 percent a year, which is nearly the same rate at which its overall world sales have been increasing.

West Germany — one of our close friends — is by far the leading Western nation in trade with the Sino-Soviet bloc. West German exports to bloc countries in 1962 were valued at $749.9 million. Britain was in second place — although not a close second — with exports to Communist countries amounting to $393 million in 1962. France followed with exports worth $313.4 million, and the figure for the United States — consisting largely of surplus food sales to Poland under Public Law 480 — stood far below at $125.1 million.

Our allies have made it plain that they propose to expand this trade, in nonstrategic goods, wherever possible. West Germany, in the last 16 months, has exchanged or agreed to exchange trade missions with every country in Eastern Europe except Albania. Britain has indicated that she will soon extend long-term credits to Communist countries, breaching the 5-year limit which the Western allies have hitherto observed. In the light of these facts, it is difficult to see what effect the tight American trade restrictions have other than to deny the United States a substantial share of a profitable market.

The inability of the United States to prevent its partners from trading extensively with the Communist bloc is one good reason for relaxing our own restrictions, but there is a better reason: the potential value of trade — a moderate volume of trade in nonstrategic items — as an instrument for reducing world tensions and strengthening the foundations of peace. I do not think that trade or the nuclear test ban, or any other prospective East-West accommodation, will lead to a grand reconciliation that will end the cold war and usher in the brotherhood of man. At the most, the cumulative effect of all the agreements that are likely to be attainable in the foreseeable future will be the alleviation of the extreme tensions and animosities that threaten the world with nuclear devastation and the gradual conversion of the struggle between communism and the free world into a safer and more tolerable international rivalry, one which may be with us for years and decades to come but which need not be so terrifying and so costly as to distract the nations of the world from the creative pursuits of civilized societies.

There is little in history to justify the expectation that we can either win the cold war or end it immediately and completely. These are favored myths, respectively, of the American right and of the American left. They are, I believe, equal in their unreality and in their disregard for the feasibilities of history. We must disabuse ourselves of them and come to terms, at last, with the realities of a world in which neither good nor evil is absolute and in which those who move events and make history are those who have understood not how much but how little it is within our power to change.

Suggestions for Additional Reading

From its inception NATO has inspired a vast outpouring of books, articles and pamphlets which shows no sign of abating. Inevitably, most of the literature is ephemeral, concerned with immediate military or technical problems, which lost their significance once the problem had been solved or the event left behind. In the early years of NATO especially, leading journalists examining NATO as a news event often provided the most penetrating insights into the organization. Notable among this group are Drew Middleton, *The Defense of Western Europe* (New York, 1952), Walter Lippmann, *Isolation and Alliance: An American Speaks to the British* (Boston, 1952), and Theodore H. White, *Fire in the Ashes: Europe in Mid-Century* (New York, 1953), all of which works regard NATO as a savior of Western civilization. The two most important studies of NATO in the early years, which examined its present and future from the vantage points of the United Kingdom and Canada respectively, were the Royal Institute of International Affairs, *Atlantic Alliance: NATO's Role in the Free World* (London and New York, 1952) and the Canadian Institute of International Affairs, *Bulwark of the West: Implications and Problems of NATO* (Toronto, 1953). There is a bibliographical review of the early years of NATO in Lawrence S. Kaplan, "NATO and Its Commentators: The First Five Years," *International Organization*, VIII (November, 1954), pp. 447–467.

NATO has intrigued political scientists as a laboratory for the evolution of a new kind of international organization or as a new arena for America in world affairs. Among the contributions are John A. Krout, ed., "The United States and the Atlantic Community," *Proceedings of the Academy of Political Science*, XXIII (May, 1949), and Ernest M. Patterson, ed., "NATO and World Peace," *Annals of the American Academy of Political and Social Science*, CCLXXXVIII (July, 1953). Most analytical studies by political scientists have concentrated on a politico-military approach, with the military utility of the alliance emerging as the major criterion of NATO's value. Arnold Wolfers, ed., *Alliance Policy in the Cold War* (Baltimore, 1959); Robert Strausz-Hupé, William R. Kintner and James E. Dougherty, eds., *Building an Atlantic World* (New York, 1963); Francis O. Wilcox and H. Field Haviland, Jr., eds., *The Atlantic Community: Progress and Prospects* (New York, 1963); and Edgar S. Furniss, ed., *The Western Alliance: Its Status and Prospects* (Columbus, 1965) characterize this approach. Perhaps the best of this genre is Klaus Knorr, ed., *NATO and American Security* (Princeton, 1959), with most of the contributors employing the tools of the behavioral sciences to find solutions to the problem of security.

Many NATO observers have regarded the organization as a stepping-stone toward a European union or a new regional organization. M. Margaret Ball, *NATO and the European Union Movement* (New York, 1959), relates NATO to the numerous functional organizations involving Europe and America that had sprung up after the war, but suggests dangers in confusing form with substance. More optimistic are Christian Herter, *Toward an Atlantic Community* (New York, 1963), and Kurt Birrenbach, *The Future of the Atlantic Community*

(New York, 1963). Balancing this optimism is the perceptive book of Robert Kleiman, *Atlantic Crisis: American Diplomacy Confronts a Resurgent Europe* (New York, 1964), which strikes a Gaullist note in dampening expectations of an Atlantic Union, blaming the United States for inability to understand the changing Europe of the 1960's, Richard J. Barnet and Marcus G. Raskin, *After Twenty Years: The Decline of NATO and the Search for a New Policy in Europe* (New York, 1965), go even farther and feel that the future of Europe and of world peace require an American disengagement from Europe. Henry A. Kissinger, *The Troubled Partnership: A Reappraisal of the Atlantic Alliance* (New York, 1965), offers a middle ground: Kissinger sees a future as well as present need for NATO, but notes the contradictions and confusion, internal and external, which beset the alliance. It is noteworthy that, with all the literature on NATO, the vast bulk of it is political or military, with too little attention given to the economic problems of the organization. Ronald S. Ritchie, *NATO: The Economics of the Alliance* (Toronto, 1956), attempts to redress the balance.

Historians have approached NATO warily and in much fewer numbers than political scientists. Massimo Salvadori, *NATO, a Twentieth-Century Community of Nations* (Princeton, 1957), provides a useful collection of documents, most of them concerning international organizations that may be considered predecessors of NATO. Karl W. Deutsch *et al., Political Community and the North Atlantic Area* (Princeton, 1957), compares an analysis of NATO with early experiments in alliances, to see what prospects NATO has of avoiding the fate of past organizations. The two most

satisfying histories to date are Ben T. Moore, *NATO and the Future of Europe* (New York, 1958), and Robert E. Osgood, *NATO: The Entangling Alliance* (Chicago, 1963), but both are primarily concerned with military and strategic problems.

Research centers such as the Foreign Policy Institute of the University of Pennsylvania, the Woodrow Wilson Center of International Relations at Princeton, the Washington Center of Foreign Policy Research of Johns Hopkins, and the Mershon Center for Education in National Security of Ohio State University have been responsible for some of the above works in addition to shorter monographs on specific issues of NATO. In response to the continuing interest in NATO older journals emphasizing NATO questions such as *International Organization, World Politics,* and *Orbis* have been joined in the 1960's by more specialized organs such as *NATO Letter,* the *Atlantic Community Quarterly* and *Western World.* Additionally, each member nation has official publications which define the relationship between it and the organization. The Department of State from time to time publishes reviews of the United States and NATO. The most ambitious publication has been *NATO: The First Ten Years, 1949–1959* (Washington, 1959), although its text does not fulfill the promise of the title.

One of the more valuable means of understanding the inner life of NATO will emerge from publication of memoirs, letters, and autobiographies by its founding fathers and by public figures — military and political, European and American — involved in its history. A few have already appeared. It is reasonable to expect that primary sources of this kind will be increasingly available as NATO approaches its twentieth anniversary.

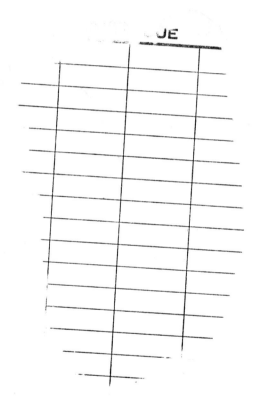

DUE